SUCCESSFUL
FAMILY
BUSINESSES

QUEENA N. LEE-CHUA

SUCCESSFUL
FAMILY
BUSINESSES

*Dynamics of Five Filipino
Business Families*

ATENEO DE MANILA UNIVERSITY PRESS

ATENEO DE MANILA UNIVERSITY PRESS
Bellarmine Hall, Katipunan Avenue
Loyola Heights, Quezon City
P.O. Box 154, 1099 Manila, Philippines

Cover design by Fidel Rillo
Book design by Jon Felix F. Malinis

The National Library of the Philippines CIP Data

Recommended entry:

Lee-Chua, Queena N.
    Successful family businesses:
dynamics of five Filipino
business families / by Queena
N. Lee-Chua. - Quezon City:
ADMU Press, 1997
    1v

    1. Family-owned business
enterprises - Philippines - Case
studies. I. Title.

HD62.25P5 1997 338.73'09599 P973000180
ISBN 971-550-246-6 (pbk.)

Contents

PART III   THE FAMILY, THE BUSINESS

Preface

My quest for a book on the Filipino family business that takes into account family dynamics and its psychological underpinnings has taken the best part of a year. I encountered difficulties and there were times when I wanted to concentrate instead on less time-consuming issues such as those related to math—my specialty.

What situations created the most difficulty for this book? The very nature of the family business itself precludes studying mere strangers. Random sampling, which is ideal for any statistical research, had to be ruled out for the simple reason that would-be respondents may not be amenable to intensive interviews. All the five families, purposively selected and studied, are either personal friends or friends of friends.

The time factor is also cogent. These families own businesses, and cannot spend precious time "chatting" with a researcher. Therefore, the question-and-answer portion had to be launched almost immediately. Yet, the interview sessions could not be rushed and typically lasted for about 2½ hours per person in each company. I was fortunate enough to have had established good rapport with almost everyone (with the help of Dr. Jacinto Gavino of AIM in some cases) so that each interviewee was generally willing to discuss sensitive issues.

Not all information I gathered, though, are for public consumption. In two of the families interviewed, I had to refrain from writing about "juicy bits" (which would bolster some conclusion or another) because they had specifically requested that those be kept off the record. No recording machines were allowed to run and I had to keep shorthand notes that I transcribed the moment I arrived home.

The feeling of voyeurism was almost always in the air. I had to remind myself that I was doing an exploratory study and not conducting a therapy session. At times, especially during group interviews, when things would get more explosive and people would begin to blame one another, I had to intervene, but not too much, else they would clam up altogether. A paradigm of basic clinical learning goes: Never open a can of worms unless you are capable and ready to put them back in. If I had probed further and uncovered deep and sore wounds, I should have been, by all respects, available to do therapy at once. Anything less would have been unethical.

There are rewards despite all the difficulties. Aside from contributing in some way to the fields of psychology and business, I have learned a few lessons on how my own family's business should be managed more effectively. Because these are real-life cases in a down-home context, insights and experiences of interviewees have helped enrich me more than a dozen case-study books written abroad could. In the process, I have come to appreciate even more deeply the resilience and perseverance of local family corporations.

Without the sympathy and encouragement of some colleagues, this book could never have materialized. They are, of course, to be properly acknowledged: Dr. Jacinto Gavino, who started me on the exploration of family dynamics; Dr. Honey Carandang, who guided me all the way; Dr. Miren Intal, who recommended that I focus on successful families instead of dysfunctional ones; Dr. Allen Tan, who suggested a sensible division of contents; Fr. Jaime Bulatao, S. J., who helped me see the value of empirical experiences; Dr. Robert Beavers and Dr. Buck Hampson, who generously permitted the use of their scales.

Without the cooperation of all the families in this study who willingly shared their time and themselves during the interviews, this book could have lacked a most essential component. Their identities will remain unknown, however, since their names have been changed in the book. Several colleagues gave valuable help: Mr. Ricky Mercado lent me his own print and video references; Mr. Darwin Yu provided me with business materials; and Ms. Vina Relucio gave me invaluable contacts and tips on genograms.

Acknowledgements are also due Ms. Esther M. Pacheco, director of Ateneo Press, for her perseverance in wanting to see my work in book form and for her publisher's eye in making sure that my work becomes more understandable to the lay reader; Ms. Benilda R. Escutin for her painstaking editing of the book; and members of the Ateneo faculty and administration, especially at crucial moments.

I also want to thank my friends, who accepted the time I spent with the book and away from them; my father William, who related his experiences and some anecdotes about family business; my brother Garrick, who wrestled with the computer when it threatened to run amuck; my sister Portia, who kept the house running while I was doing this book; and my mother Anita, in whose memory this work is dedicated.

I

FAMILIES IN BUSINESS

FAMILY CORPORATIONS TODAY account for a significant volume of industry. [1] As in any other type of business, a family business experiences problems of profit generation, asset acquisition, and employer-employee relations. Certain issues are, however, inherent to family-owned businesses, and research done by the Asian Institute of Management (AIM) has identified three especially pertinent areas: balancing familial with professional expertise, choosing a successor, and solving inheritance problems (Quintos 1992).

To deal with these issues, more than 50 family-business centers have been organized in the United States since the 1960s, mostly affiliates of university business schools or independent resource consultants (Fenn 1994).

They have tried to address these issues through the business perspective, but most have eventually discovered that the psychological underpinnings of familial dynamics cannot be ignored (Cohen 1974;

---

1. Alcorn (1982), for instance, says 98 percent of the millions of corporations in the U.S. are not controlled by industry giants, but maintained by family firms.

Dyer 1986; Rosenblatt et al. 1985). Although some of the research done touches on psychological factors, one that explores familial dynamics in depth still needs to be done.

Research on family corporations in the Philippines is almost nonexistent. A number of case studies are found in theses, but these are mostly analyzed from the viewpoint of business management, and the psychological issues are seldom, if ever, touched upon (Quintos 1992).

This book aims to make a more empirical delineation of the issues at hand. After perusing a sample of 18 cases written by undergraduates for a course in family business at the Ateneo de Manila, I have identified four psychological themes to be most common, i.e., they appear in at least four of the cases. In order of frequency, they are: (1) individuation, or the assumption of responsibility for one's own actions, happiness, and goals in life; (2) power; (3) sibling rivalries and alliances; (4) in-law relationships; and (5) nonfamily, professional concerns.

These areas are of course not isolated; each is inextricably linked with the others—necessitating a systems approach. Even if problems crop up in the midst of seemingly "business" concerns, they may be rooted in family dynamics.

The Family Systems Approach

The family is not made up of isolated individuals going their own separate ways, for whatever one does affects the others as whole, and a myriad of relationships exists. The family is an interactional system of behaviors, processes, and relationships viewed as a functional whole (Andolfi 1979). Therefore, to understand the individual, we must delve into the family system, and vice-versa (Bowen 1978; Gurman and Kniskern 1980; Minuchin 1987).

The main aim of families, as with other groups, is to maintain homeostasis, and it is in this process that problems may arise. Individuation and power themes, roles and alliances, sibling rivalry, and other nuclear and extended family problems may be present in one degree or the other. A family systems framework, which takes these factors into account, provides a more thorough understanding of the workings of the family. Espousing this view are Andolfi (1979), Minuchin (1987), and Hansen and L'Abate (1982). In the Philippines they include Carandang (1987) and a host of other researchers—Castro (1992); Liwag (1987); Nisperos (1984); Tuason (1992)—who have studied families using this framework.

While different theories on family systems abound, I have chosen the framework offered by family therapist W. Robert Beavers, who affirms that family functioning is best described on a continuum rather than as discrete topologies (Beavers and Hampson 1990). Beavers's concepts are complementary to Bowen's (1978) differentiation of self and Minuchin's (1987) structural concepts.

Beavers measures competence of whole families according to current task performance, and examines the structure of the family, its mythology, goal-directed negotiation, autonomy, and family affect. These concepts I shall explain in detail later in this chapter.

Beavers classifies family styles as (1) centripetal, (2) centrifugal, and (3) mixed. The centripetal family looks inward to its members for satisfaction. It is concerned with social approval and presentation; it encourages dependence on the family. Its members are physically close, and it discourages aggression and negative feelings inconsistent with the family myth. The centrifugal style family looks outside (of the family) for satisfaction. It ignores dependency on its members. It shows aggression and conflict, and is unconcerned with appearances and social approval.

A combination of the two is the mixed style, and the centripetal or centrifugal style operates depending on the situation and the members involved. Thus, the whole family can be described more comprehensively according to competence and style. It is only after making this assessment that therapy can proceed.

Although Beavers's scales, which determine competence and style, have been validated time and again in the United States and in other areas (Lee 1988), they have not been put to systematic use in Philippine research.

I have chosen not to research on dysfunctional families, and instead look at families more positively. I shall analyze families successful in business. (Whether they are also successful in their personal lives remains to be seen.) The strategies they have employed can have useful implications for both family therapy and business applications.

The Family Firm

A family business may range from the neighborhood Mom and Pop store to the multinational. For the purposes of this study, I have defined a family firm as one wherein at least 50 percent of the ownership and management falls within one family—whether related by blood or marriage.

The concept of role confusion plays a key role in each area to be discussed. Studies have shown that business and family matters often overlap (Dyer 1986; Lansberg 1983; Levinson 1971; Rosenblatt et al. 1985) as, for instance, in discussing the family business over the dinner table or carrying over *tampo* (peevishness) to the workplace.

While textbooks advocate a delineation of family and business matters, and list a host of cogent reasons for doing so (Lansberg 1983; Mancuso and Shulman 1991), my study is hinged on the premise that family and business relationships are intertwined. To what extent, this book aims to answer. Furthermore, it proposes that therapy on the family as a system may benefit the business as well.

After discussing in detail the five areas—individuation, power, sibling rivalries, in-law relationships, and nonfamily professional concerns—I present a general assessment of family functioning in both the home and in the workplace. In this regard, I attempt to answer two questions. What is the level of each family's health and competence? What relation, if any, does this have in business functioning?

In the West; in the East

It has been estimated that, in the United States alone over 90 percent of all corporations (including 35 percent of *Fortune's 500*) are either owned or controlled by a family (Lansberg 1983). The average lifespan of the family firm is only 24 years, which is coincidentally also the average tenure of the founders of the firm. Approximately 70 percent of the firms are either sold or liquidated after the death or retirement of the founders (Beckhard and Dyer 1983).

The succession issue has so troubled a number of management consultants that they have tried various methods to ensure smooth transitions. A popular notion among them is that of culture—the basic assumptions, shared meaning, and pattern of expectations shared by the organization's members (Dyer 1986; Lank 1992). Culture can be transmitted through the structure of the organization itself, formal statements of organizational philosophy, explicit reward systems, criteria for the selection or promotion of employees, stories and myths about key people and events, leader reactions to critical incidents, even the design of physical space (Dyer 1986).

Drawing from the notion of culture, some researchers have examined the overlaps between the family and its business, which is also a main issue in this book. They have approached this issue, though, from the management, not the psychological, point of view.

Lansberg (1983) succinctly summarizes the issue in this way: Institutional differences between family and business stem from the fact that each exists in society for fundamentally different reasons. The family's primary social function is to assure the care and nurturance of its members, and relations are thus meant to satisfy each member's developmental needs. On the other hand, the fundamental aim of business is the generation of goods and services through organized task behavior, and relations are guided by norms that facilitate this end.

Such qualities as innovativeness, aggressiveness, and intelligence have been found to be traits of entrepreneurs who have founded businesses (Fritz 1992). Good founders and owners have certain functions: They contain and absorb risk, stimulate innovation, hybridize new assumptions, and embed other noneconomic values.

To ensure that such goals are met, many families hire consultants to assist them in strategic planning—developing a family mission statement, a conceptual mission model, key programs and objectives (Covey 1989; Ward n.d.) Many families though, resist the notion of planning, which they deem rigid, time-consuming, and totally unnecessary. When the firm grows and outsiders increasingly have shares at stake, governance is usually coursed through a board of directors.

Most of the literature deals mainly with strategies for successful succession planning, and their methods range from hiring consultants to holding conferences among themselves (Donnelly 1964; Dyer 1986; Levinson 1971; Mancuso and Shulman 1991; Vancil 1987). The different methods of transition—appointing an heir apparent to hiring outside managers to going public on the stock market—are debated hotly. None of the approaches can be considered the ideal one, since there are advantages and disadvantages for each.

Because of the rise of Asian newly industrialized countries (NICs), some Western researchers have begun to realize the merit of certain Eastern notions, questioning the validity of their own management principles, such as the notion that business should remain "strictly business." Robinson (1964, 139) notes:

> Certain values long held at least in verbal awe in professional management circles may not be universally valid. The concept of *complete neutrality* [emphasis mine] in interpersonal relations may not, after all be conducive to the most effective communication with a large organization . . . [as illustrated by] the Japanese experience.

As for the allegedly "unprofessional nature" of many Asian enterprises, certain ingenious methods (based on social and cultural control) have been developed to surmount possible problems. Of the Chinese accounting system, for instance, Limlingan (1986, 161) says:

The Chinese businessman has traditionally used the cash-flow system of accounting in contrast to the double-entry system. Its simplicity has also meant an inadequate control system. The Chinese solution is to rely on social control (e.g., family ties) to augment the weak formal control system. In addition, Chinese firms have relied on their own social organizations (the Chinese Chamber of Commerce as credit bureau) and on their social customs (payment of debt during the Chinese New Year), and even on the modern commercial banking system (postdated checks) to facilitate their business operations.

Perhaps the most intensive research on Asian businesses has been conducted by AIM professor Leonardo Silos (1992) who has studied the bureaucracy and the clan. He uses the term *oikos* (the Greek word for house, household, or family), which is multifaceted:

It is the root word of the English term economy, drawing out the economic component of the house, a connection that surfaces whenever we call business establishments "house" of such and such a family, the house of Morgan, the house of Mitsui, and so on. *Oikonomia* (economy), on the other hand, meant household management and a *oikonomos* (economist) was a house administrator, a term also used generally for administrator or manager. *Oikos,* then, also conveys the idea of management . . . . Thus, *oikos* suggests central themes that make up the subject matter of our inquiry: organization, management, authority, family, and economic orientation of the house. It conveys the dual concern for the household and its economy, reflecting the concern of the business firm for the business and its organization (Silos 1992, 1).

Drawing from sociology and economics, Silos attempts to delineate the distinctions between clan and bureaucracy, and to show that these two concepts, at first glance irreconcilable, can actually be integrated in the Asian context. The particular mix of clan and bureaucratic cultures produces a flavor unique to Asian corporations, and Silos cites the case of the hugely successful Japanese firms, wherein these two notions work in tandem. Drawing from Leibenstein's (1987) work, he puts Japanese and Western firms side-by-side, and argues that both work quite well in their own environments.

Aside from the Japanese, the Chinese have also been studied. Limlingan (1986, 136) draws upon Redding's work in comparing Western and Chinese systems which he finds similar.

What do these comparisons augur for our study? Since most of the research frameworks used by such authors as Limlingan and Silos are Western, they find largely similar management patterns in the Eastern and Western business firms. Still there are fundamental differences between East and West, and we must try to develop an indigenous perspective in studying our own Philippine system.

Recently, the *Far Eastern Economic Review* came out with a series on Asian family dynasties. Stories included the development of Korea's Hyundai (Clifford 1994); Taiwan's Chinfon (Baum 1994); Indonesia's Salim, the major stockholder in First Pacific (Silverman 1994); and the Philippines' Aboitiz clan (Tiglao 1994). Asian family businesses are now getting the attention they need.

In the Philippines the only available literature on family corporations—aside from occasional stories on the ups and downs of companies like San Miguel or entrepreneurs like the French Baker—have been those written by management graduate students (Caruncho 1976; Garcia 1973; Henson 1975; Quintos 1992), with Limlingan (1986) comparing the Chinese and the Filipinos with others in the Southeast Asian region.

Businessworld researchers (Belleza et al. 1995) have just published interviews with next-generation leaders (mostly, sons of prominent local tycoons), which, however, lacked data analysis. Silos (1992) conducted studies on Asian business contexts, but included no actual case studies. This book is therefore the first to delve in-depth into the psychological dynamics of the Filipino family business.

The family business as defined in this book is one in which at least 50 percent of management and ownership belongs to one family related by blood or marriage.

Using the case study method and the family systems approach, I analyze the nuances of both family and business systems, clinically describing the patterns that evolve.

The Families Studied

I focus on five families who all run successful businesses. Some of these cases have been provided through the Asian Institute of Management (AIM) researchers; some through my own contacts.[2]

I have defined "a successful business" as one that has existed for at least 10 years, is still existing, and has made a name for itself in its field. The founder may still be alive, and thinking of succession; the second generation may already be in charge; or the third generation may even be running the business. Approximate annual earnings and growth will be given in the individual case studies.

Family businesses have problems inherent in their very nature, and this leads to the premise that these issues are intertwined with familial ones. To get a more comprehensive picture of these relationships, I have had to draw out the perceptions of each family member involved in the business. The focal variable therefore is the perception of each member toward family functioning as a whole, and toward the family situation in business.

The focal variable—perception—will be addressed according to the following subvariables: (1) individuation, (2) power, (3) sibling relationships and other alliances, (4) in-law and other extended family relationships, and (5) professional and other nonfamily issues.

Individuation is the degree of enmeshment/fusion or differentiation of a member from the family or the business system. The more individuated the individual is, the more autonomous he or she is. *Power* refers to the dominant or controlling force in the family or the business system. *Sibling relationships and other nuclear family alliances* include the (usually informal) partnerships—duos, triads, triangulations—which arise and are maintained in the context of the nuclear family in their personal or

---

2. I ruled out random selection, since many families refused to be interviewed (for reasons of sensitivity and secretiveness), and only those willing were selected for interviews. All the families selected have businesses based in Metro Manila, and all the corporations have been existing for at least 10 years. Two are purely Filipino-owned and managed, others are Filipino-Chinese or Filipino-Spanish, but most are Filipino citizens.

business lives. *In-law and other extended family relationships* involve either formal or informal relations that arise and are maintained when in-laws and other relatives enter the family and the business. *Professional and other nonfamily issues* are those involving members unrelated to the family by blood or marriage such as professional managers. These variables will be discussed at length in the section on family dynamics.

For comprehensive family assessment, I have had to use multiple methods of gathering information both overt and covert (Herbert 1988), namely: (1) questionnaire, (2) in-depth semistructured interview, (3) genogram, (4) the Beavers Self-Report Family Inventory, (5) the Beavers Interactional Scale of Family Competence and Style, and (6) Dyer's 12-point checklist. I gave a questionnaire (see appendix 1) to each family member currently involved in the business—founder, co-founder, children, siblings, other relatives, and others. The questionnaire served to gather demographic data such as the members' name, age, gender, status, citizenship, position in the firm, educational attainment, work history (religious affiliation, if needed). I also gave the questionnaire to each professional nonfamily member occupying a decision-making position.

I conducted an in-depth semistructured interview (see appendix 2) with each family member in the business who was willing to be interviewed. For my purposes, the ideal interviewee was the "top" or the "second-to-the-top" manager and nonfamily member occupying a decision-making position.

The interview guidelines (see appendix 2) were based on the five key areas—individuation, power, sibling relations and other nuclear family alliances, in-law and other extended family relations, and professional and other nonfamily issues. The interview provides a flexible means of obtaining and verifying information.

I provide a genogram for each family, graphically summarizing the pertinent relationships among family members. I also present a family business chart that graphically encapsulates the relationships in the hierarchy. This way the two instruments can be compared and contrasted.

The Beavers Self-Report Family Inventory or SFI (see appendix 3) was given to each family member currently employed in the business. The SFI aims to elicit the perceptions of each member about the workings of the family. The responses, coded along a continuum, provided quantitative data for family functioning, and provided a basis for my own observations and conclusions.

The items in the Beavers Interactional Scale of Family Competence and Style were coded, based on interviews, questionnaires, genograms, and SFIs. These were graded qualitatively or along a continuum, as was appropriate and, on the basis of Beavers's guidelines, the family was classified on its competence and style. I then compared this classification to the dynamics in the family business while discussing similarities and differences. Items in this scale are discussed in detail in the next section.

In order to assess the health of the business, I used Dyer's (1986) 12-point checklist. Though not exhaustive, the checklist helps provide a clue to the future functioning of the business. (Dyer's checklist is detailed in the next section). I then compared and contrasted the business health scores (à la Dyer) with family health scores (à la Beavers).

Family Dynamics

Two major forces, says Bowen (1972), continually operate within the family: the force toward togetherness and the force toward individuation. The first is instinctive, deeply rooted in living species, evolving because of our need to band together for survival. Manifested in many different groupings such as races, social classes, gender divisions, and religious cults, this togetherness force has proven functional through time. It defines all family members, says Papero (1983, 139), "as alike in terms of their basic perspectives, principles and feelings." It is further manifested, continues Papero, "in the degree to which people adapt self to preserve harmony with another, the degree to which one person will assume responsibility for another and will define his or her role in life on the basis of relationship, rather than on principle, and the degree to which one automatically thinks and defers to another before self."

Some Western psychologists object to this type of togetherness as being too much of a good thing. Bowen (1978), for instance, compares the family to an electronic circuit, each member connected to all the others, sending and receiving signals through the system. If the family is too fused, the reaction of any member, whether positive or negative, is transferred to all the others. When anxiety arises, everybody begins to act in predetermined, almost instinctual patterns, what Bowen terms the "emotional reflex."

In efforts to maintain familial equilibrium, there may inevitably develop neuroses and psychoses, pseudo-partnerships, and triangles.

Individuation

Given the pitfalls of too much togetherness, it is no wonder that Bowen and his colleagues laud individuation, or the person's assumption of responsibility for his or her actions, happiness, and goals in life. One avoids blaming others for personal failure, and is capable of setting attainable goals based on principles carefully thought out, without prejudice from the family, or being unduly influenced by one's emotions. A truly individuated person is his or her own person, so to speak, and yet can experience genuine caring for others, since he or she feels no need or anxiety to overwhelm others, and has enough self-integrity not to be overwhelmed. This is "rooted in an instinctual drive to be a self-contained, independent organism, an individual in one's own right" (Kerr 1981, 236), and can only truly emerge when anxiety within the family is reduced.

In working with family businesses, Rosenblatt (1985, 243) notes that individuated families also experience disappointment or anger. However, members will be able to cope and not fear rejection when they disagree. He compares the individuated and enmeshed thus:

> In a family that has achieved individuation, or among family members who have done so, working together in the business would allow them freedom to differ from one another and even freedom to go their separate ways without punishment, retaliation, or an end to interaction. They would not be tied to the business. However, where individuation has not been achieved or still an issue in family struggles, relations in the business may be tense in several ways. A sort of dictatorship may exist, in which the boss tells others what to do and they simply do it, or there may be recurrent struggles over control, goals, rights, duties, credit and other issues, with arguments and feelings running at several levels.

Can a person be too individuated? One can be too "independent" and "uncaring" toward the family, what Minuchin (1987) calls *disengagement.* Here, the individual exhibits inappropriate, rigid boundaries and virtually lacks loyalty to the family. "Total independence" is not really what individuation means.

Take the centripetal and centrifugal forces that are closely tied to family cohesion or disengagement. According to Stierlin (1974), the centripetal force is associated with high family cohesion—everyone is pulled toward an intellectual and emotional oneness. The centrifugal force tends to push members away from the system. What we have to keep in mind, though, is that both forces are functional at different stages—what becomes pathological is when only one predominates all of the time.

The degree of differentiation and individuation, however, often depends on culture. Confucian-oriented countries, for instance, strive toward harmony. "The pursuit of the key virtues—righteousness, wisdom, fidelity, filial piety, propriety—helps people maintain inner harmony and at the same time enhances harmoniousness in social relations" (Westwood 1992, 49). Instead of relying on laws, for example, the Chinese often rely on hierarchical relationships, and seldom question their status. What the West may view as autocratic or undifferentiated, the East may simply accept as the natural order of things.

Individuation has become fashionable, especially among the younger generation. Still, it is not binding. Westwood (1992, 126) elaborates:

> Children are taught to be conforming, dependent and deferential. Such characteristics tend to be viewed rather negatively in the West, where children are taught to be independent, questioning and individualistic. In Southeast Asia, they are part of a natural and necessary orientation for the maintenance of a complex and intricate social system.

And the East does have its advantages—just witness the burgeoning newly industrialized Asian dragons. Successful businesses can result sans Western-style individuation.

This is important for therapists to understand. Having worked with many Chinese families, Jung (1984, 369) cautions that "lacking knowledge of cultural differences will mislead many therapists to incorrectly diagnose what is basically a cultural difference as something that is pathological." Writing about Taiwanese families, Tu (1991) agrees. Observing Japanese family corporations, Silos (1991) makes similar observations.

The genuinely individuated individual is flexible—neither too near nor too far. And so it is with the family. Katy, the wife of renowned family business consultant Danco (1981, 234), should know:

> Sometimes it's good to run alongside each other. At other times, it may be the best thing to take different paths. Having a common goal doesn't mean we have to use the same paths to get there. It's necessary, sometimes, and even enjoyable to run the way we want, at our own paces.

Two Beavers SFI Subscales are pertinent to our individuation variables: *cohesion* and *emotional expressiveness*.

Cohesion, say Beavers and Hampson (1990, 59) is "related to competence and includes items originally designed to measure self-ratings of family style (centripetal-centrifugal). The items on this scale involve satisfaction and happiness through togetherness and emphasis on family closeness."

On a scale of 1 to 5, where 1 denotes that the statement is most applicable to the family, and 5 the least (R denotes that scoring should be reversed.)[3] Four items on the Cohesion Subscale are shown below.

#2	:	Our family would rather do things together than with other people.
#15	:	Our happiest times are at home.
#19(R)	:	Family members go their own way most of the time.
#27(R)	:	Our family members would rather do things with other people than together.

---

3. All subsequent subscales follow this scoring system except when otherwise indicated.

(The fifth item has its own range.)

#36: On a scale of 1 to 5, I would rate independence in my family as:

| 1 | 2 | 3 | 4 | 5 |

| No one is independent. There are no open arguments. Family members rely on each other for satisfaction rather than on outsiders. | Sometimes independent. There are some disagreements. Family members find satisfaction both within and outside of the family. | Family members usually go their own way. Disagreements are open. Family members look outside of the family for satisfaction. |

Scores are added for all five items, and the sum classified as in the table below.

Scoring and Classification of Family Responses for the SFI Cohesion Subscale

SFI Sum	Equivalent	Classification
	1	Optimal
5	2	
	3	Adequate
10	4	
	5	Midrange
15	6	
	7	Borderline
20	8	
	9	Severely dysfunctional
25	10	

SOURCE: Beavers and Hampson (1990, 211).

Emotional expressiveness is also related to overall family competence. It "involves perceptions of feelings of closeness, physical and verbal expressions of positive feelings, and the ease with which warmth and caring are expressed by family members" (Beavers and Hampson 1990, 59).

The five items on the <u>SFI Emotional Expressiveness Subscale</u> are:

#1	:	Family members pay attention to each other's feelings.
#9	:	Our family members touch and hug each other.
#13 (R)	:	Even when we feel close, our family is embarrassed to admit it.
#20	:	Our family is proud of being close.
#22	:	Family members easily express warmth and caring toward each other.

Scores are added for all five items, and the sum classified this way:

Scoring and Classification of Family Responses for the SFI Expressiveness Subscale

SFI Sum	Equivalent	Classification
	1	Optimal
5	2	
6		
7		
8	3	Adequate
9		
10	4	
11		
12		
13	5	Midrange
14		
15	6	
16		
17		
18	7	Borderline
19		
20	8	
21		
22		
23	9	Severely dysfunctional
24		
25	10	

SOURCE: Beavers and Hampson (1990, 211).

We can also compute for <u>Family Style</u> scores: centripetal, centrifugal, or mixed. The three SFI items include:

> #4 : The grownups in this family understand and agree on family decisions.
>
> #14 : We argue a lot and never solve problems.
>
> #27 : Our family members would rather do things with other people than together.

The formula for SFI Style is as follows (Beavers and Hampson 1990, 210):

$$\text{SFI Style} = (\underset{\#14}{\_\_} \times -.25) + (\underset{\#4}{\_\_} \times .30) + (\underset{\#27}{\_\_} \times .22) + 2.11$$

Styles are classified as in the table below.

Scoring and Classification of Family Responses for SFI Style

SFI Style	Classification
1	Centripetal (CP)
2	Moderate centripetal (MCP)
3	Mixed (M)
4	Moderate centrifugal (MCF)
5	Centrifugal (CF)

SOURCE: Beavers and Hampson (1990, 43-47).

Power in the Family and in the Business

The family is primarily looked upon as a system involving power relations and a governing process (Haley 1976). The main issue is one of control, and the interrelationships revolve around these questions: What kinds of behavior take place ("What are the rules?"), and who controls what takes place ("Who sets them?").

Interestingly, most psychologists feel that this situation is inevitable. Hansen and L'Abate (1982, 103) affirm:

> Just as it is impossible not to communicate, it is also impossible not to engage in this struggle for control over the definition of the relationship. Every time that a person speaks (or fails to speak), that person is inevitably indicating what kind of relationship he or she is in, either by directly defining it or by counteracting the other's definition. Any message is simultaneously a report and a command. Even the "helpless" person in reporting his or her helplessness is at the same time commanding the other to take charge.

Be that as it may, Haley (1962) has likened the family system to a thermostat, where there is a pre-existing homeostasis. Once something occurs that moves familiar behavioral patterns outside the usual ones, then power—overt or covert—usually intervenes to restore balance. In this sense, power is seen neither as positive or negative, but is part of the normal state of affairs.

Taking the systems view, Olson and Cromwell (1975, 5) define power as "the ability (potential or actual) of an individual(s) to change the behavior of other members of a social system."

Family power has three domains: bases, processes, and outcomes. *Bases* consist of the individual's resources which he or she can use to control a given situation. Drawing from research, Raven and his colleagues (1975) identify six common bases: (1) *legitimate,* based on normatively prescribed rights; (2) *referent,* based on one's identification with or attraction to the powerful one; (3) *expert,* based on one's awareness that the other has more knowledge or skills in a particular area; (4) *informational,* based on another's superior persuasive capabilities; (5) *reward,* based on the gratifications the other controls; and (6) *coercive,* based on the other's capability to inflict punishment or negative outcomes.

Processes refer to the interaction and relationships among family members during various stages of "discussions, decision-making, problem-solving, conflict-resolution, and crisis management" (Olson and Cromwell 1975, 6).

Applied to the business context, the issue of power becomes more complex. In most family firms, the founder typically heads both business and family systems (Lansberg 1983, 41). Because he is the head of both spheres, crises are magnified when they arise. "He or she often experiences personal psychological difficulties as a result of the conflicting pressures. Founders frequently experience a great deal of stress from 'internalizing' the contradictions that are built into their jobs as heads of the family firm." These contradictions revolve around problems of selection, compensation and equity, appraisal, training and development, oftentimes resulting in nepotism.

Power is also intricately tied up with the issue of succession. There have been countless tales of the founder's unwillingness to let go of the reins, for fear of losing power. This can be related to a personal loss of identity, fear of loss of significant work activity, fear of loss of influence, even fear of mortality or impending death. Analyzed in this fashion, it comes as no surprise that succession becomes a thorny issue. Sonnenfeld (1985, 285) classifies the different exit styles of heads of firms as the (1) monarch; (2) ambassador; and (3) governor.

The *monarch,* who is completely dedicated to the business, tends to create order amidst external turbulence. He possesses a great gift for institution-building, as well as for looking after growth in sales, assets, employees. He usually obtains long-term support from stockholders, and assumes personal responsibility for problems. However, "he is often restless in tranquil periods; stubbornly defends old strategies; de-emphasizes profitability; exits due to instability of the firm; lacks outside management models; and is reluctant to develop the next generation."

Notable examples include Lew Wasserman of the MCA, Lenore Hershey of the *Ladies Home Journal,* J. P. Morgan, J. P. Getty, and George Eastman of Kodak.

The *general,* who is attached to his leadership identity, bridges internal factions and is ready to return to the office during crises. He can build strong top leaders but is nevertheless cautious in leadership transitions; he tends to show resistance to the successor, even undermining his own.

William Paley of CBS, Robert Woodruff of Coca-Cola, and Harold Geneen of ITT are prime examples.

The *ambassador* is well-informed on management styles other than his own and cultivates interests outside the business. He tends to overstay, eager to share his wisdom in the office. He can also accept assignments to represent the firm elsewhere.

However, he tends to be meddlesome, offering unsolicited advice or public comments, and making confusing statements on executive roles. These may distract his successor from the company. Furthermore, his behavior may encourage fads detrimental to the firm.

Thomas Watson Jr. of IBM, Winthrop Knowlton of Harper and Row, Irving Shapiro of Du Pont, Roger Hill and Richard Damon of the Bank of Boston displayed ambassadorial departure styles.

The *governor* usually does not stay long in the company, a stable and formal bureaucracy, even though it offers more opportunities. He maintains a wide range of outside business interests. Unthreatened, his successor is free to revamp his (governor's) own strategy. Upon retirement the governor cuts himself off from the firm. Unfortunately, the firm may not perform well during his term. Because of his broad outside interests, he is often distracted from his office responsibilities and does not train his successor well enough.

Governors include Walter Mack of Pepsi-Cola, Douglas Fraser of United Auto Workers, Thornton Bradshaw of RCA, Reginald Jones of General Electric, and David Rockefeller.

Different cultures vary in their perception of power. Asians generally respect and accord legitimate power to their parents and other elders, accepting the hierarchical division as normal. In many Filipino families, the father is the power, although in some cases, this is exercised by the mother, or in her or the father's absence, the *kuya* (older brother) or *ate* (older sister) (Miranda 1991). In dealings with others, the family stresses *utang-na-loob* (debt of gratitude), *amor propio* (self-esteem), and *hiya* (shame).

In Confucian-oriented societies, patrimonial power is accepted and perceived as natural. Filial piety reigns as do mutual obligations and reciprocity. Westwood (1992) believes that the Southeast Asian style includes a dependence orientation by subordinates, personalism, moral leadership, harmony building, conflict diffusion, aloofness and social distance, didactic leadership, yet paradoxically, respect for dialogue.

The important point to be raised here is that in the Asian context, the exercise of power does have different implications, not necessarily negative, either from the family or business sense. In *Oikos*, Silos (1991, 117-18) defends paternalism as a style, devoting chapters to tracing its historical growth in great detail, and concluding by defending it from its Western detractors.

> The negative "ism" is of relatively modern origin. Modelling the exercise of authority after the household head, being traditional and "natural," had required no further deliberation or legitimation. The negativity of paternalism was evoked in contrast to and in the process of legitimatizing another emerging type of authority [democratize] in modern times. The context was polemical.

Silos concludes that the proof that a paternalistic power structure can work effectively lies in the emerging Asian dragons of today, where business and family are both considered significant.

Studying Taiwanese enterprise, Tu (1991, 118) makes similar observation. He explains:

> Some scholars view the "father-figure" leadership style as the major reason that the family enterprises cannot be modernized in Taiwan. Before we jump to that conclusion, however, we should ask an obvious question, "Why has the family form of leadership been so widely adopted by Taiwan's enterprises?" The reason is that this structure does not exclude legalistic styles of administration, while simultaneously promoting a feeling of human warmth *(renging)* to which people in Taiwan are accustomed. Owners act not only as regulators who enforce a system of regulations, but also as people who can bend the rules when necessary. If these family-style owners/managers want to control their employees efficiently, they must understand clearly that in the process of enforcing regulations, they almost must necessarily consider the morale of their employees and work to gain their trust.

Keeping this in mind, we can look to the Leadership Subscale of the SFI for validation. Beavers and Hampson (1990, 59) view leadership here in the positive sense. They explain that this "involves ratings of strong and consistent patterns of adult leadership in the family (whether shared or single); this scale also corresponds well with overall competence, in that healthier families show higher leadership patterns."

The three items on the <u>Leadership Subscale</u> are:

#8 (R)	:	There is confusion in our family because there is no leader.
#16	:	The grownups in this family are strong leaders.
#32	:	One person controls and leads our family.

The scores are added, and the sum classified as in the table below.

**Scoring and Classification of Family Responses
for the SFI Leadership Subscale**

SFI Sum	Equivalent	Classification
	1	Optimal
3	2	
	3	Adequate
6	4	
	5	Midrange
9	6	
	7	Borderline
12	8	
	9	Severely dysfunctional
15	10	

SOURCE: Beavers and Hampson (1990, 211).

Sibling Relations and Other Nuclear Family Alliances

Three basic relationships exist in every nuclear family unit: spouse-spouse, parent-child, and child-child. "Family interaction is a dynamic arena in which spouses affect each other, parents affect children, children affect parents, and siblings affect each other" (Schvaneveldt and Ihinger 1979, 456).

As we have seen, following Bowen (1972), marital relationships are largely influenced by the degree of differentiation and apartness, and their ways of coping with these. The resulting relationship has its own power base, and subsequent interactions are largely influenced by these dynamics.

Ideal relationships are characterized by cohesive parental coalitions, wherein decisions are agreed upon jointly by spouses, and communicated clearly to the children in a consistent manner. The reality hardly matches the ideal, however. When stress threatens the marital relationship, special alliances—what Bowen (1972) terms *triangles*—inevitably form.

When the level of anxiety is low, relationship between spouses appears stable, but with heightened tension, one of the partners may become uncomfortable and attempt to move out, forming another relationship with an outsider, generally a child. The partner left out from the original twosome may react in either of two ways: relief, which strengthens the newly-forged alliance, or anxiety which attempts to restore the original one. In this case, he or she may, in turn, act positively by making a peace overture and by promising to make amends, or negatively by issuing threats or being jealous. Disruptions normally occur.

What happens to the new alliance? If the original partner (one of the spouses, for instance) leaves the new pair alone, then the parent-child dynamics may take on a more intensive hue. Papero (1983, 143) illustrates:

> In a mother-father-child triangle, for example, tension may develop in the marital pair with the greater discomfort located in the mother. She in turn manages her anxiety by focusing on the child. She may become exceedingly protective of the child, her worry about the child's health may intensify, or she may become openly critical and fall into conflict with the child. The tension in the marital relationship dissipates as the intensity of the mother-child relationship increases.

Triangles are seldom static. Alliances are forged and broken, sometimes with rapidity; at other times they remain stable for years until the next crisis. The more individuated the individual members are, the less likely will the triangular interrelationships lead to family dysfunction. Too much enmeshment tends to cause entanglements within triangles (Bowen 1972). However, the other extreme may also hold: If power is not clearcut, many small alliances for or against certain family members are formed, resulting in disarray of interlocking relationships. This brings us to the relationships among the siblings themselves.

Traditionally, sibling relationships have been the least researched. In an extensive review, Schvaneveldt and Ihinger (1979, 453) lament that so little conceptual, empirical, and theoretical attention has been given to the experiences children share with siblings, which have a profound influence on their socialization and personality development processes.

Research on the only-child syndrome is even sparser. The few studies on children focus mainly on birth order focusing on the eldest child. And to emphasize its vital role, birth order has been linked with achievement, affiliation, conformity, mental illness, anxiety, dependency, personality, domination, protectiveness, leadership, and others (Toman 1961).

Among the studies made on achievement, Adler's (1928) is one of the most highly regarded. He suggests that the eldest, being an only child before another one comes along, revels in the almost total attention showered on him. When the next child is born, some of the attention is given to him and in an attempt to regain his privileged status, the eldest (elder) becomes strongly motivated to achieve.

Perhaps because the more positive roles are adopted by the eldest, later-born children may often assume negative roles in an effort to get attention, to differentiate (Bossard and Boll 1960). Conversely, this theory has likewise been advanced to explain why parents tend to spoil the youngest. Family researchers believe that with the last child, parents realize that they are nearing the end of their parenting roles, and tend to hold on, enthroning the youngest in the position the eldest once occupied (Latts 1966).

Bowen (1976, 87) has capitalized on this and boldly states that nothing can be more significant than "knowing the sibling position of people in the present and past generations." Inevitably, Bowen's systems framework includes birth order.

Bank and Kahn (1975, 319-21) identify certain functions siblings perform for each other. *Identification* refers to "the process by which a sib sees himself in the other, experiences life vicariously through the behavior of the other, and begins to expand on possibilities for himself by learning through a brother's or sister's experience." This tends to promote fusion and dominance by one sibling, and may occur when neither parent exerts a dominating influence.

Differentiation, the opposite process of identification, occurs when distantiation is desired. This may also occur when no parent is dominant, and other siblings perceived to be different. A defense mechanism, this may serve as "a way of externalizing or projecting deeply felt needs or anxieties."

Mutual regulation denotes the process by which siblings serve as "sounding boards" and "testing grounds" for each other. They "provide an 'observing ego' for one another that can exert an effective and corrective impact upon, and for, each other. The mutual regulatory process among brothers and sisters proceeds on the basis of fairness and honest relationship among relative equals." Neither sibling is perceived to be dominant although usually, there is one acknowledged power. The influence he or she wields, nevertheless, is accepted by everybody as perfectly legitimate.

Direct services are the day-to-day exchange of goods and services among siblings including teaching skills, lending money, controlling resources, and so on. The more direct services are exchanged, the greater the sibling solidarity.

Dealing with parents is a process usually performed through coalitions, such as balancing (colluding with a parent or another sibling to equalize forces in conflict situations), keeping secrets or tattling (a measure of sibling loyalty), translating (a go-between process by which siblings "increase the degree of family openness as they filter and channel issues from the broader culture into the family complex" (Schvaneveldt and Ihinger 1979, 460). The process may be small-range, as in helping parents understand "baby talk," or wider in scope, as in getting parents to understand "generation-X"); and pioneering (where one sibling initiates an act, in the process modelling and giving permission for the others to follow; and can be positive, as in the eldest getting high grades in school; or negative, as in the eldest taking drugs).

How about sibling power? Our previous discussion of Raven's (1975) typology also applies here. Legitimacy may be based on age, sex, parental command, or societal norms. Referent power is closely tied up with identification. Expert power may come about through perceived intellectual, physical, or moral capacities. Reward or coercive power may be utilized when siblings have different resources.

A cogent issue is the concept of fairness. In terms of family, fairness means ideally that no one sibling is treated "better" than the rest. Fairness in this context is generally equated with equality. Many parents have agonized over perceived inequities and try to standardize reward and punishment methods. Very often, though, the eldest or the youngest is seen to be the family favorite, and repercussions usually set in.

These family interactions frequently arise once more in business relationships. Triangulation often occurs (Rosenblatt et al. 1985) and decision-making may prove problematic. Power struggles among siblings, especially those pertaining to succession and inheritance, have been the fodder of cafe gossip all over the world.

After studying a number of brother-brother business dealings, Levinson (1971) concludes that ordinarily, the eldest tends to be the successor, and usually treats the others condescendingly. In return, the younger brother tries to compensate by carving out a niche for himself in the business, and guarding it closely. Brothers tend to have equal shares on the board, but arguments erupt, notwithstanding.

How about equity? Here we may have to differentiate between family and business. What may be "fair" in the family context is not applicable in the firm.

In the family, fairness in the vertical relationship between parents and children is based on need. Parents have an accepted moral and societal obligation to provide for their children. In horizontal relationships among siblings, as we have said, fairness normally connotes equality, with uniform allocations for all.

However, fairness in business is often said to stand on merit. Siblings may not receive exactly equal salaries, for instance, but these differences are seen to be a function of some other factors such as expertise, commitment, and performance which everybody perceives as valid. Problems arise when not everybody shares similar perception.

Once again, we have to situate our discussions within the Philippine context. Here, there exists an accepted hierarchy among siblings, with the kuya or ate as the accepted leader, enjoying more privileges, yet being saddled with more responsibilities than the others. Gender may also interfere, especially in the business context, where daughters are sometimes passed over as successors in favor of their brothers, even when the brothers are admittedly less qualified.

Menchik (1980) found that for entrepreneurs, sons, not daughters, are usually considered valid successors. Incompetence is seldom the main reason, but cultural socialization patterns and the loss of the family name when the daughter marries are generally used as justification.

Beavers and Hampson (1990) give no subscale specifically for sibling relationships because they view them as part and parcel of familial ones. Taking the three alliances as a whole (spouse-spouse, parent-child, child-child) though, we can validate family functioning by using the conflict subscale.

Conflict is "related to competence, in that 'healthy scores' indicate low levels of overt unresolved conflict, fighting, blaming and arguing, with higher levels of negotiation and acceptance of personal responsibility in solving conflict situations" (Beavers and Hampson 1990, 59).

The 12 items in the <u>SFI Conflict Subscale</u> are given below.

#5 (R)	:	Grownups in the family compete and fight with each other.
#6	:	There is closeness in my family but each person is allowed to be special and different.
#7	:	We accept each other's friends.
#8 (R)	:	There is confusion in our family because there is no leader.
#10 (R)	:	Family members put each other down.
#14 (R)	:	We argue a lot and never solve problems.
#18 (R)	:	We usually blame one person in our family when things aren't going right.
#24 (R)	:	One of the adults in this family has a favorite child.
#25 (R)	:	When things go wrong, we blame each other.
#30 (R)	:	The mood in my family is usually sad and blue.
#31 (R)	:	We argue a lot.
#34	:	Each person takes responsibility for his or her behavior.

Scores are added for all 12 items, and the sum classified as in the table below.

**Scoring and Classification of Family Responses
for the SFI Conflict Subscale**

SFI Score	Equivalent	Classification
	1	Optimal
12	2	
18	3	Adequate
24	4	
30	5	Midrange
36	6	
42	7	Borderline
48	8	
54	9	Severely dysfunctional
60	10	

SOURCE: Beavers and Hampson (1990, 211).

In-Law and Other Extended Family Relationships

The nuclear family does not exist in a vacuum. At all times, it is surrounded and buffeted by outside forces, constantly testing its adaptability, flexibility, and openness to change. Peer groups, community circles, in-laws, grandparents, and the rest inevitably affect family functioning. Rueveni (1979) believes that viewing a family solely as an independent unit may prove misleading. He suggests a social network approach, which includes other people who maintain important and ongoing relationships with the members.

In-laws occupy a special place in the extended family. Though unrelated by blood, they soon assume significant positions within the family circle, and inevitably influence its workings either positively or otherwise. In a stable family, where boundaries are flexible, parent-child relationships excellent, siblings affectionate and caring, and the personality and background of the prospective in-law in harmony with that of the parents and other siblings, the entry of the in-law may even be welcomed by all.

If one of the factors is missing, the in-law may have a more difficult time being accepted. If, for instance, the parent may, for one reason or another, not feel like "letting go" of the child, then the in-law may be perceived as an interloper, a usurper, often treated with hostility and mistrust. Classic cases of mothers clinging on to their sons while mistreating their daughters-in-law illustrate this situation. When sibling relationships are chaotic, the presence of an in-law can exacerbate the tension. Even when the bond between parent and child, or sibling and sibling is cohesive, it can be disrupted when a child insists on marrying somebody unacceptable to the family (e.g., of a different race or religion, or of an "unsuitable" family).

When we factor in the reality of a family business, the situation becomes more complicated. Aside from personal worries, the in-law has to contend with the overlaps between the new family and the new business. Often, the in-law is a contender for a top management position, fueling jealousies from the founder's children. At the same time, the in-law is often treated as a "second-class" citizen, with little attention paid to his or her own feelings and needs, all of which are supposed to be surrendered to the family he or she has entered into by marriage.

> It is the rare owner who appreciates how hard it will be for an in-law to feel fulfilled by a career in the family business. Many times, in-law parents/owners adopt the attitude of benefactors, as though they have granted the in-law a tremendous gift unattainable anywhere else (Speck and Attneave 1973, 37).

At compensation time, the in-law usually gets the short end of the stick. Often, he or she is rewarded not so much on the basis of job performance but on the relationship to the daughter or son. This may flag the in-law's morale. Mancuso and Shulman (1991) are blunt:

> Many times, parents/owners have publicly extolled the value and commitment of sons- or daughters-in-law, even stating the in-law was easier to work with than the blood children. Yet, when the time comes to distribute the will or stock in the company, the same owners have been reluctant to adequately compensate the hardworking in-law.

The daughter-in-law has special problems. Often she is perceived as an intruder, especially if her husband does not perform well, or is unhappy in the business. She may be used as a scapegoat for the family's frustrations over her husband's behavior. In many Asian countries, where females are relegated to a secondary role, the situation becomes magnified. This state of affairs is unfortunate, because when dealt with fairly and tactfully, an in-law can prove invaluable for company growth.

For one, the in-law comes into the firm as a relatively mature outsider, without the biases and emotions which may interfere with the assessment of relationship between parents and siblings. "The brother-in-law never saw his brother-in-law as a helpless infant, or his mother-in-law as a loving, protective parent. He may be a step ahead of the family's own children in becoming an effective, unbiased manager" (Mancuso and Shulman 1991, 37).

Closely tied to this is the next factor: The in-law is freed from individuation problems within the family. The mother who tends to be protective of her son may retard his growth in the company, covering up for his mistakes or insisting that he be paid an inflated salary.

> Parents carry mental pictures of their children—how they looked on their first day of school, what it was like to comfort them when they fell playing, having to constantly remind them not to talk to strangers or play with matches. In many family businesses, parents/owners try too hard to protect their successor candidates from failure and pain, simply because this protection is what the parent is accustomed to providing. They fail to see that denying successors the right to make mistakes and suffer the results retards their growth. In this regard, in-law children have a distinct advantage (37-38).

For another, in-laws do not normally possess the feeling of being entitled to the business just because they have become "part of the family." Studies show that many of them work doubly hard to be accepted.

Within the Asian paternalistic, extended-kin family context, in-laws and other relatives particularly are often preferred over nonfamily members because they are believed to be more trustworthy, loyal, and committed (Westwood 1992). They enhance family cohesion resulting in increased productivity.

No SFI subscale measures extended family relationships, although there may be a correlation between family cohesiveness and permeability to outsiders. We can, therefore use the Cohesion Subscale as a tentative measure here.

Professional and Other Nonfamily Relationships

Professionals and nonfamily members form a significant part of what Boissevain (1974) calls a family's effective zone. When the family business wants to expand, or the would-be heir is seen as not interested or incapable of handling the business, the founder may decide to hire skilled outsiders. Making this decision is often crucial, and may revitalize or seriously damage the firm.

Differences between the professional and the "original/traditional" leadership include (Dyer 1986) *new leadership patterns*. With extensive education and training, professionals normally pride themselves in their accounting, finance, and marketing skills. In many cases, they hail from backgrounds different from the rest of the other employees. Founders are committed to the firm, taking risks when necessary while professionals tend to be more cautious, and put their career above all else.

Add in the factor of personality. Silos (1991, 149) puts it picturesquely:

> The slow, roundabout, intricate and delicate patterns of [the founder] are a source of frustration to professionals, who know they have in their bag of tricks more efficient ways of dealing with problems. The family, on the other hand, usually will not tolerate professional behavior that does not respect the family code, often unspoken.

Add in the element of mistrust. In his study of Asian firms, Redding (1990) argues that many family companies are reluctant to hire outsiders because they feel that there can only be bounded and limited trust in nonkin relationships.

An interesting facet of management in Asia is the difference between two management styles: problem-solving versus situation-accepting. Many professionals in Asia have been trained in the Western method (Silos 1991) which focuses on problem-solving (Adler 1986). This may conflict with the traditional way of doing things.

Another source of difference is *new psychological contrasts between management and workers*. In contrast to founder figures, who are usually seen as charismatic or father figures, professionals may be construed as too impersonal, too cold, too bureaucratic. Founders normally exhibit more than a business relationship with their workers—bonds are virtually familial. These founders support employee picnics, attend employee weddings, and even be *ninong* (godfather) or *ninang* (godmother) to employees' children.

With professional managers, though, the link is generally utilitarian, and employee commitment depends on salaries, bonuses, and performance. The familial touch is often missing, replaced by objective accounting methods.

New organization-community relations is another factor. Founders generally grew up in the community where their businesses are established, and therefore feel attached to it. They may become active in several associations, and use their organization for the benefit of the community or local parish. With professional managers (who usually come from other areas) at the helm, community considerations are normally cast aside. No preferential treatment is given (to the community).

They may also differ in their view of *organizational effectiveness*. Concerned about company growth and profits, professional managers normally see things on short-term, and want quick results, which may cause chaos in the company, good financial results notwithstanding. Dyer (1986, 107) remarks:

> Because many professional managers enter a family business during a crisis period, they feel great pressure to get quick results and turn the company around. Decisions are often made to fire or lay off employees or to sell parts of the business that are not profitable. They are less concerned with product development and innovation and devote most of their energy to improving the company's financial picture.

Still, there are decidedly certain advantages to hiring professionals. As we have seen, they can be instrumental in ensuring company growth and expansion, thereby maintaining the wealth of the family. A source of expertise, professionals can act as buffers to family influence, especially as a hedge against nepotism (Davis, Gallo, and Leach 1990). Danco (1979, 211) remarks:

> I've seen some sad cases where the owner-founder continually waits and assumes that his prodigal children are going to reform their ways and return to the fold to take up their dutiful management of the company ... This may make a nice parable in the scriptures, but in business it tends to be a disastrous fantasy.

Outsiders can train the next generation, and are less emotionally involved with the firm (Davis et al. 1990).

In a recent review of American family businesses, Ehrenfeld (1995) concludes that the most successful ones are, in some way, professionalized. He contends that they have become automated, more competitive, more resourceful, more planned, and can draw from more experiences.

For the professionals, entering a family firm has its merits: They get quick exposure to a wide variety of decision-making situations, they acquire the power to get things done quickly, they have a good opportunity to learn from and interact with the owner himself.

Professionals can also be broadly classified into these categories: (1) The *superstar* is loyal and competent, (2) the *transient* is not loyal but competent anyhow, (3) the *family retainer* is loyal although incompetent, and (4) the *parasite* is not loyal besides being incompetent (Davis et al. 1990).

After professional management arrives, the founder may be more amenable to going public. This move does satisfy some objectives: to increase personal wealth, to diversify, to obtain equity capital for expansion, to attract and motivate employees, to avoid taxation of company assets, to satisfy investment bankers, and so forth (Dyer 1986).

Still, public ownership can have some negative, albeit unexpected, consequences: Conflict can erupt among executives and family members; the company becomes focused on short-run results, such as stock prices;

the founders may resent public scrutiny; a negative change in power may occur; and there is always the risk of a takeover (Dyer 1986). As with the decision to hire professionals, the decision to go public has to be discussed and thought over carefully with all parties involved.

Nepotism is another source of contention among Westerners. Almost all Western management consultants denounce the preferential hiring of relatives as a practice ill-suited to a "modern" company which is based on principles and merit. They argue that this breeds jealousy, lowers the morale of nonfamily employees, and pressures the founder to hire incompetent family members (and makes it difficult to fire them).

Paradoxically enough, Western management consultants seem to forget that nepotism does have it benefits: Family members tend to be more adaptable, more interested, and stay longer.

Many business enterprises in Asia, like those of Koreans and Japanese, are filled at the top by senior management who are blood relatives (Yoo and Lee 1987)—and they have become quite successful. Nepotism here is not judged as wrong, but is even expected by subordinates as well as leaders.

What about justice and equality for all? Perhaps the adage "everybody is equal, but some are more equal than others" applies here. For the family business system is unique in several ways, one of them being—yes—in the practice of nepotism. Alcorn (1982, 208) argues this point frankly:

> The business is to serve as a vehicle for family enjoyment and betterment. If this is so, then logically, decisions about the management and perpetuation of the business must take family ties into account. For the founder to name a relative as successor over the heads of more experienced but nonfamily members is *not* [emphasis mine] unjust. It is a decision perfectly in keeping with the underlying principle of the business . . . .
>
> A family business should, as a matter of justice, give preference to family members. The owner should be straightforward about this and not mislead people with hogwash about how "we play no favorites here." If no family favorites are played, it is not a family business. Nonfamily

employees are thus forewarned. Certainly, some good potential employees may be lost to the firm because they prefer not to have the family standing in the way of their advancement. There is nothing wrong with their declining such jobs; what is wrong is to take the job and then constantly moan about unfairness.

As previously noted, there are no SFI subscales for measuring permeability of the family to outsiders, but the family Cohesion Subscale may be a good item to keep in mind.

Functioning of the Family and of the Business

To take one more look at the families and summarize interactions from a more wholistic viewpoint, let us categorize them through Beavers's and Hampson's (1990) typology. They use the <u>Interactional Scales of Family Competence</u>, which focus on several areas:

1. *Structure of the family.* This refers to the power relationships and leadership pattern in the family.
   a) Overt power. At the lowest level of power relationships, *chaos* represents a "high degree of entropy and low levels of effective leadership related to task performance" (Beavers and Hampson 1990, 14). Adaptation to changes is practically nil.

      On the next level, there is *marked dominance* by one or two members. Often rigid and authoritarian, the dominant member controls a situation which he or she fears may become chaotic if left alone.

      Moderate dominance shows a more egalitarian structure, and at the *led* level, there is increasingly direct and respectful development toward shared leadership.

      At the *egalitarian* level, shared leadership between parents is characterized by flexibility in adapting to different situations.
   b) Parental coalitions. This refers to the result of the relationship between parents and between parent(s) and child(ren). At the lowest end of the scale, a *parent-child coalition* forms when one or both parents have entered into reciprocal relationships with one

child, either by overt side-taking or by a covert need for affirmation, depending on the style of the family (Beavers and Hampson 1990.)

At the midpoint, a *weak parental coalition* vacillates from strong to nonexistent, but is evidently inconsistent.

At the highest end, a *strong parental coalition* forms when both parents complement each other in their roles, and generational boundaries are clearly defined. Disagreements are usually kept to the couple, without enticing allegiances from any child.

c) Closeness. At the lowest end, *amorphous, vague, and indistinct boundaries among family members* comprise the norm. Generational and interpersonal boundaries are often violated, and a sense of individuality is lacking. Following Bowen (1978), this state is called undifferentiated ego mass which is often evidenced by verbal invasion (parents speaking on child's behalf, for instance), and can be pathological (incest, for example).

At the midpoint, individuals exhibit *isolation, distancing* behaviors in an attempt to differentiate from the family. Boundaries are more distinct, but at the cost of great effort.

At the highest level of functioning, *closeness with distinct boundaries among members* characterizes the family. Greater spontaneity occurs with greater individuation, yet paradoxically, there develops deeper and more genuine intimacy, as the individual learns to be autonomous, and at the same time, capable of being close to the family.

2. *Mythology.* This refers to the family's conception of its behavior and relationship vis-a-vis the outside world. Each family certainly has its own myth (e.g., we are an achieving family; we are a happy family) and this scale measures the congruence of the family members' perceptions with each other.

The scale goes from *very incongruent* to *somewhat incongruent* then *neutral* to *mostly congruent* then *very congruent.*

3. *Goal-directed negotiation.* This refers to the family's ability to deal with problems related to either task performance or emotional matters. This involves a myriad of factors: the number of family members actually cooperating, the time it takes to achieve a goal, the emotions of the members while participating, and so forth.

This scale goes from *poor* and *extremely inefficient* to *neutral,* then *good* to *extremely efficient.*

4. *Autonomy.* This refers to the family members' ability to accept and acknowledge responsibility for their own or others' actions or feelings.

    a) Clarity of expression. This factor is based on several issues: To what degree are members encouraged to speak their mind, so to speak? How clear is this expression? How does the family deal with ambivalence? At the end is the least competent level, *hardly anyone is ever clear,* groupthink may even dominate, out of fear or hopelessness on the members' parts.

    At the midpoint, individual expression is *somewhat vague and hidden,* and may vacillate between expressing and keeping silent on certain issues. Spontaneity is not the rule, and even if ambivalent issues may be hinted at, they may not be expounded on.

    At the most competent end of the scale, expression is *very clear,* and members are encouraged to express their thoughts and feelings without fear, while respecting others. There is a sense of spontaneity, with less monopolizing and more active exchange between members.

    b) Responsibility. This refers to the degree in which members acknowledge personal responsibility for their actions both inside and outside the context of family relations.

    At the lowest end, *members hardly, if ever, voice responsibility for individual actions.* Denial and forgetting are usual avoidance tactics with some families blaming and attacking others.

    At the middle, *members sometimes voice responsibility for individual actions, but tactics include blaming others sometimes, speaking in the third person or plural.* A common statement is, "I can't believe we have a son/daughter who would even think about doing __" (Beavers and Hampson 1990). Often, secrets regarding transgressions of parties can be held over each other's heads.

    At the healthiest end, *members are regularly able to voice responsibility for individual actions.* There is less blaming or distortion; there is openness, trust, respect for rule.

    c) Permeability. This refers to the degree to which members are receptive to the verbal and nonverbal messages of others. At the lowest end, *members are unreceptive,* or indifferent toward others.

    With the moderate ratings (*members frequently unreceptive* and *moderately open*), individuals are more often placed in predetermined role relationships, with responses automatically received or discarded.

At the highest end, receptivity is *open,* and members acknowledge each other's messages quite well.

5. *Family affect.* This refers to the expression of feelings, mood and tone, and conflict resolution within the family.

a) Range of feelings. At the lowest level, there is *little or no expression of feelings*; a sense of sadness or despair often envelops the family. It seems as if the members feel nothing they do will create an impact—sometimes, guarded cheerfulness rules, thereby restricting the expression of potentially negative feelings.

At the next level, *although some feelings are expressed, most feelings are masked.*

Higher up is the *obvious restriction in the expression of some feelings,* then *direct expression of many feelings with some difficulty.*

At the top of the scale is the *direct expression of a wide range of feelings.* Expression of feelings is seldom restricted, and negative issues are not sidestepped. Humor is a frequent tool.

b) Mood and tone. At the lowest level, the mood is *cynical, hopeless, and pessimistic.* There is often a sense of "no way out."

Only a little better is the next level—*depressed,* then *overtly hostile,* characterized by ambivalence.

At a higher level is *politeness, without impressive warmth or affection* or *frequent hostility with times of pleasure.*

At the highest end, the tone is *usually warm, affectionate, humorous, and optimistic.* Even during tough times, the family manifests confidence that it can cope.

c) Unresolved conflict. Conflict is inevitable in families, and its resolution ranges from coercion to compromise and negotiation.

This scale measures the impact of conflict on group functioning, ranging from *severe conflict with severe impairment of group functioning,* to *definite conflict with moderate impairment of group functioning,* to *some evidence of unresolved conflict without impairment of group functioning,* to *little or no unresolvable conflict.*

At the high end *(little or no unresolvable conflict),* the family is usually characterized by higher levels of clarity, permeability, closeness, and so on.

d) Empathy. This refers to "one person's accurate reception, understanding, and response congruent to another's emotional overture, and a resultant joining and sharing of those feelings" (Beavers and Hampson 1990, 29). This definition can easily be extended to the family level with each member's ability to empathize being analyzed.

At the low end, empathy is *grossly inappropriate with regard to feelings,* manifested either overtly (opposition) or covertly (indifference).

At the next level, there is a marked *absence of any empathic responsiveness.* Rolling eyes when another is talking is a frequent indication.

At the middle level, there exists *attempted empathic responsiveness, but failure to maintain it.* Empathy here usually seems forced.

Higher up is *generally empathic responsiveness with one another, despite obvious resistance.* (At least the effort is there.)

At the highest level is *consistent empathic responsiveness,* which facilitates communication.

6. *Global health-pathology scale.* This is the only scale with a 10-point continuum. It attempts to summarize the overall functioning of the family, from *most pathological* to *healthiest,* based on the factors given above.

Beavers (1990) classifies the family into one of several categories: optimal (1 or 2 rating), adequate (3 or 4 rating), midrange (5 or 6 rating), borderline (7 or 8 rating), and severely dysfunctional (9 or 10 rating).

The Beavers and Hampson Health/Competence Subscale

Family members' views on health and competence can also be assessed by the SFI Competence Subscale which Beavers and Hampson (1990, 59) explain as

> The largest and principal scale [and] corresponds with the global competence ratings . . . . The themes addressed in this scale are those of happiness, optimism, problem-solving and negotiation skills, family love, strength of parental (or adult) coalitions, autonomy/individuality emphasis, and minimal blaming/increased responsibility patterns.

The scoring of responses to the items on the SFI Competence Subscale ranges from 1 to 5, where 1 denotes that the statement is most applicable to the family, and 5 least applicable. The 10 items on this subscale are:

#2	:	Our family would rather do things together than with other people.
#3	:	We all have a say in family plans.
#4	:	The grownups in this family understand and agree on family decisions.
#6	:	There is closeness in my family but each person is allowed to be special and different.
#12	:	In our home, we feel loved.
#15	:	Our happiest times are at home.
#16	:	The grownups in this family are strong leaders.
#17	:	The future looks good to our family.
#18 (R)	:	We usually blame one person in our family when things aren't going right.
#19 (R)	:	Family members go their own way most of the time.
#20	:	Our family is proud of being close.
#21	:	Our family is good at solving problems together.
#24 (R)	:	One of the adults in this family has a favorite child.
#25 (R)	:	When things go wrong, we blame each other.
#27 (R)	:	Our family members would rather do things with other people than together.
#28	:	Family members pay attention to each other and listen to what is said.
#33	:	My family is happy most of the time.

(Two other items have their own range.)

#35	:	On a scale of 1 to 5, I would rate my family as:

1	2	3	4	5

My family functions well together.

My family does not function well together at all. We really need help.

> #36 : On a scale of 1 to 5, I would rate the independence in my family as:
>
> | | | | | |
> |---|---|---|---|---|
> | 1 | 2 | 3 | 4 | 5 |
>
> | 1 | 2 & 3 | 4 & 5 |
> |---|---|---|
> | No one is independent. There are no open arguments. Family members rely on each other for satisfaction rather than on outsiders. | Sometimes independent. There are some disagreements. Family members find satisfaction both within and outside of the family. | Family members usually go their own way. Disagreements are open. Family members look outside of the family for satisfaction. |

Scores are then added for all 12 items, and the sum classified as in the table below.

**Scoring and Classification of Family Responses
for the SFI Health/Competence Subscale**

SFI Score	Equivalent	Classification
	1	Optimal
19	2	
29	3	Adequate
38	4	
48	5	Midrange
57	6	
67	7	Borderline
76	8	
86	9	Severely dysfunctional
95	10	

SOURCE: Beavers and Hampson (1990, 211).

The Family Business Checklist

What about healthy businesses? This study has aimed to analyze successful family businesses; successful is broadly defined as the company's having existed for at least 10 years, having attained a certain growth, and having been recognized as one of the top in its field. In this sense, all the corporations studied are successful.

Furthermore, we can systematically predict <u>business functioning</u> by using the checklist developed by long-time family management consultant Dyer (1986, 158):

1. Are the family and its leaders aware of the problems and tradeoffs that they are now facing or will face in the future?
2. Has the family planned for future family and business needs?
3. Is there a well-thought-out management succession plan, and has it been communicated to the relevant parties?
4. Has the family developed an ownership succession plan that complements the management succession plan?
5. Do the leader and the successors have an interdependent relationship?
6. Does an effective training program exist for future leaders of the business?
7. Do members of the firm (both family and nonfamily) share similar views of equity and competence?
8. Do family members work together collaboratively to solve problems?
9. Has the family created successful mechanisms for managing conflict?
10. Are there high levels of trust among family members as well as among family and nonfamily employees?
11. Do the leaders have feedback mechanisms (outside board members, consultants, effectiveness measures) to tell them when they are off course or are ineffective?
12. Does the family have a "balanced perspective" when making tradeoffs between family needs and business needs?

With Beavers's scale, we can check family functioning in the home. With Dyer's list, we can check family functioning in the business. Having done these, we can then investigate possible overlaps.

CASE STUDIES

MOST SERIOUS STUDIES in psychology have focused on experiments and quasiexperiments, but recent clinical texts have suggested that the case study may in fact be the more useful tool in certain situations. Being more comprehensive and in-depth, it can be as powerful as the traditional experiment.

Recent local researches have used the case study successfully—Liwag (1987) for autistic families, and Tuason (1992) for alcoholic families, to cite two instances.

What about case studies of family businesses? Little research has been done on the psychological dynamics of Philippine family corporations, and the case studies presented in this book are therefore pioneering in the field.

The dynamics that operate in the five business families who own and manage their own business firms—Excellence Printers, Quality Shoes, Gochiamco Groceries, Inc., Snackfood Delights, and Garments House—I present in part 2 as case studies.

Findings that dwell on overlapping themes in the family system itself and in the business have surfaced through the use of several assessment tools—a demographic questionnaire, in-depth interviews, the Self Report Family Inventory (SFI), and observation. In the presentation I emphasize recurrent themes from the information I was able to gather.

The demographics (such background information as name, age, position in the family, marital status, and number of children) are represented in the genogram, while the same information (substituting position in the company for position in the family) is represented in the organizational chart of the family corporation.

I have summarized the data for each family on the Subscales from the Beavers SFI in tables, and these are complemented by information gathered from the other assessment tools, which are elaborated according to the themes of individuation, power, sibling and nuclear family relationships, in-law and other extended family issues, and issues dealing with family outsiders. For each category, I have classified the responses into either the family system or the business system, later comparing and contrasting these two. My presentation on each family deals with such issues as marital alliance, family members' exposure to business, leadership style, family culture, power structure, treatment of children, sibling relations, resolution of conflicts, involvement of professionals, treatment of nonfamily employees, the acceptance of in-laws, and position of the founder.

To summarize the findings, I assess the functioning of both the family and the business. The competence and health of the family in each sphere is highlighted with the aid of the Beavers SFI Health/ Competence Subscale, while overall functioning of the family business is evaluated through the use of Dyer's business checklist.

The Perez Family: Excellence Printers

The Perez family is made up of Jacinto (57 years old), Nora (49 years old), and their four sons, ages 29, 28, 21, and 18. The two eldest sons, Peter and Paul, are both involved in Excellence Printers; the other two are still in school.

Peter is married to Rita, who is of the same age as he. They have two children, ages 4 and 3. Paul is married to Grace, and they have an only child, age 3.

I was able to interview Jacinto, Nora, Peter, and Paul.

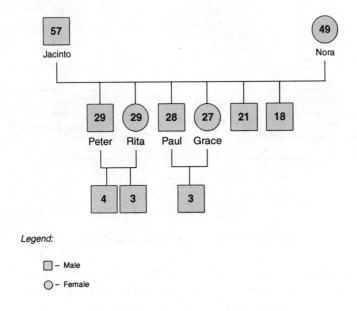

Legend:

☐ – Male

○ – Female

The Perez Family Genogram

The organizational chart of Excellence Printers shows Jacinto at the head, occupying the positions of board chairperson, company president, and general manager. Nora, second in command, is the board treasurer, company vice-president, and assistant general manager. Peter, the eldest son, is board member and concurrently production manager. Paul is also board member as well as marketing manager of the family firm.

At the bottom of the organizational chart are the staff/trainees. Among them is Grace, Paul's wife, who trains as finance officer of Excellence Printers.

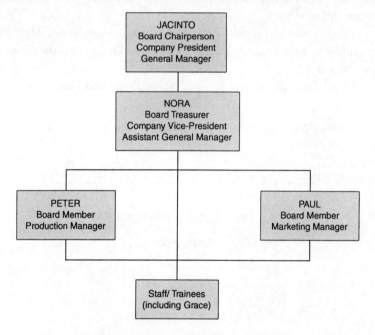

Excellence Printers Organizational Chart

In 1967, an eager editor-in-chief wanted to impress the college dean, vowing that their graduating class would come out with enough copies of the yearbook in time for graduation. With patience and determination, the young Jacinto Perez laid out the pages carefully, and visited the printing press regularly, to ensure that quality would not be sacrificed for speed. Come graduation day, each student had a copy—the first time in the history of the college, commented the dean.

This experience in printing, however, proved to have had further repercussions. A physics graduate, Jacinto veered from his vocation and decided to try his hand at printing—a completely novel experience for him then.

Armed with no more than a "great interest in printing" and a 6,000-peso loan from a rural cooperative, Jacinto bought a small letterpress machine, installed it in his garage and serviced his first clients—the departments and offices of the university he graduated from.

"That was the logical thing to do," he recounts. "Business then grew."

Jacinto, shortly after, married his college sweetheart, Nora, also a physics major. During the next two years, they had two sons in succession: Peter and Paul. (Seven years later, another son and three years later after that, still another son.)

Perhaps being a graduate of science helped shape Jacinto's interests, for he became a devotee of computers long before the fad hit Metro Manila. In 1978, he invested in a Zilog machine which he learned to program by himself.

"I had no choice," he recalls. "There were too many accounts, and I wanted to computerize the records. I felt computers would help in making everything run more efficiently."

This meant, of course, that aside from programming, Jacinto had to study accounting on his own.

"It simply had to be done."

This foresight would likewise be extended to his printing machines. He invested in state-of-the-art equipment, balancing the budget with his projections. By this time, the single proprietorship had gone into full offset operations, neccesitating more machines, all working overtime. Operations started shifting from the garage to the kitchen, and finally to separate facilities.

For the first 10 years, Jacinto worked alone. He oversaw production, marketing, distribution—a virtual one-man printing concern. Nora was busy with the children and her master's studies in physics in the state university. It was only in 1980, when she finished, that she was able to devote time to the business.

Nora started by taking on the role of accountant, relieving Jacinto of some of the pressure. She also had to learn accounting on her own, with some help from Jacinto.

The year after, Jacinto traveled to England for a printing exhibition. He combined business with pleasure, as he also took some time to view the major attractions. Perhaps it was the romance, or the sheer beauty of the place, that made Jacinto yearn for the wife he left back home.

"I missed Nora terribly. There were so many beautiful spots I wanted her to see. I vowed to myself then that it would be the last time I was going to leave her at home. Next time, she would come with me."

Jacinto asked Nora to work fulltime in the business, handle more than accounts, take responsibilities for marketing and distribution as well. Nora readily agreed.

Business was booming, and the company often received more orders than they expected. In 1983, Jacinto was one of the first printers in the country to buy an Apple Macintosh. A few years later, he and Nora decided to expand overseas by printing cards, calendars, and books, among others, for export. (England was one prime market.)

At this time, the eldest son Peter, fresh out of college with a degree in industrial engineering, expressed a wish to help in the business. The parents welcomed him and he is now production manager.

The second son, Paul, graduated with a degree in economics and decided to work elsewhere for a few years. He eventually joined the company, too, and is now marketing manager.

For more than 20 years, everything the company touched seemed to exude pure magic. Jacinto's intelligent foresight and investments in the most modern machines seemed to be worth it all. The children were helping. The wife found satisfaction in responsibilities. Little everyday spats and squabbles over schedules, clients, and services appeared to be forgotten as soon as they were over.

There was one problem the family would always remember: In the early 1990s, the workers formed a union and demanded more benefits.

Jacinto mourns: "We felt betrayed. We treated all of our employees like family. We gave Christmas parties and gifts, held company outings, and even gave a scholarship for one child in each of the families. We even paid them above minimum wage! Yet the union demanded higher salaries. You see, they were influenced by outsiders. A lot of our workers have been with us for 20 years. And, worst of all, a lot of the outsiders were relatives of my relatives."

"One was even our children's former driver. When some of the workers came to see me, they couldn't look at me straight in the eye. *Nakakasakit sa puso* (It's heartbreaking). I did not want to have anything to do with them."

It was Nora herself who negotiated with the union leaders. Finally, after four months, they reached an agreement. She put into writing the terms of the agreement (i.e., management will do this but in return you should also do that).

"Everything was spelled out," Nora explains.

Most of the union leaders subsequently left the company.

Perhaps the stress, combined with decades of toil, contributed to Jacinto's heart attack in 1993. Hospitalized and heartbroken over union demands, Jacinto decided to go into semiretirement. Nora began to have a bigger hand in the business, with the help of the two elder sons (the two younger ones are still in school, and have not yet expressed desire to join the family business).

On certain days, Jacinto drives to the office, looks over certain accounts, and deals with certain customers. He still decides over machine investments. He seems more content to let his family take over, though, even while admitting that succession is still an unresolved issue.

Are there companies held in esteem by the Perez clan? Jacinto and Nora both admire San Miguel Corporation.

"SMC started as a family corporation but now it has gone public and is run by professionals."

They hope their company can attain that status, but realize it is yet a dream, as the key positions are still held by family members.

Peter admires the efficiency of a certain printing company in Hong Kong. "Their machines are not all top of the line, but they are well-maintained."

Paul waxes enthusiastic over Ayala Corporation. *"Ang laki nila pero* smooth *ang* succession plan. *Sana ganoon ang mangyari sa amin.* (They are very big but the succession plan is smooth. I hope the same thing happens to us.)"

Excellence Printers is one of the most progressive printing companies in the Philippines, with an annual net worth of ₱400 million, including a large factory in the outskirts of Metro Manila, and another one being planned in the Subic export processing area. More than 200 employees work at the plant from glueing to stripping, die-cutting, and finishing, to delivering. Company products include world-class quality greeting cards, brochures, postcards, desk calendars, stationery, children's books, cookbooks, and magazines. Its past and present clientele reads like a list from Who's Who: San Miguel Corporation, Republic Flour Mills, Pilipinas Shell Petroleum Company, Nestle Philippines, Abbott Laboratories, Mead Johnson Philippines, Dutch Boy Philippines, Avon Cosmetics, Levi Strauss, Ace Saatchi/Saatchi Advertising, J. Walter Thompson, Basic/Foote, Cone and Belding, the Department of Tourism, Philippine National Oil Company, just to name the well-known ones.

What is the philosophy of Excellence Printers? All four family members agree: "Reliability and quality. Be true to your word, especially when you make promises to the customer. Make sure you always deliver your best."

In the Process of Individuation

The Perez couple has valued togetherness, sheltered the children and imposed discipline. All this has had lasting effect on the children, who are individuating.

Family Togetherness

"We always had time for the family," Jacinto muses. "Business was tough during the early years. It was a 24-hour job but we managed to take care of and be close to our children. Somehow, we managed."

"We always had time for the kids," Nora adds. "Even when I was helping Jacinto in the business, I made sure I tutored the kids. *Ang problema lang* (The only problem[is]), none of them got to the honor roll. That's just fine, they graduated nicely."

They went on weekly outings, heard Mass together, and had family sessions. The images evoked seem ideal. Peter and Paul agree, saying that they remain close to their parents. They bring their wives and children to their house, to the delight of Nora and Jacinto. On many Sundays, there is a gathering of the whole clan. Family togetherness indeed is prized by the Perezes.

Inspite of all the attention showered on them, the boys were a disciplined lot. Jacinto made sure that discipline was enforced when they were young.

"My mother nagged us about this and that, but it was Dad we were really afraid of. He was quiet, but as they say, still waters run deep. He was a disciplinarian," Paul reflects.

The parents claim to be fair when it came to punishing their children. "If one of them got spanked, so did the others," Jacinto laughs.

Curfew was imposed on the boys even during their college days. They were not allowed to drive until after graduation. In fact, Peter was so "innocent" that he "did not know what to do the first time he entered a topless bar."

By all accounts, the children have been sheltered. Did their teenage children resent this?

"I don't think so," Jacinto offers. "Maybe it's because they got into the right crowd; their friends were all very well-mannered. Also, we started training them when they were young, and they never complained."

Within such a protective atmosphere, were the children given opportunities to grow at their own pace? They reportedly had their own set of friends, who were readily welcomed by the family, and became sort of "family friends" *na rin* (in turn). The enforcement of discipline is emphasized, but the children understood and accepted it. However, the discipline they imposed seems inadequate for training the children for business later on.

Succession Problems

Nora harbors some misgivings. "Maybe we sheltered them too much. We should have trained them to become more independent. Jacinto and I went through some hard times, but I guess our children are luckier. They never had to work as hard as we did."

"We're having difficulty finding a successor for the business," she continues, "because the two boys do not seem to be capable enough as yet. Peter is so nice and so *mabait* (kind), that he tends to let people walk all over him. Paul is more aggressive, but he tends to be quarrelsome and argumentative; plus, he is very hot-headed." Succession is a present problem because of the overprotectiveness of one parent spilling over to the business.

Lack of Early Exposure to Business

"If there is one thing we should have done," Jacinto reflects, "it is to have started the boys young in the shop. When they were studying, they were exposed to the business, but they had no formal duties. They only got involved in this company after graduation, and even if they have been here for some years, both Nora and I feel that they cannot handle it on their own yet."

"After I got sick," Jacinto continues, "I knew I had to slow down, but Nora feels she still cannot; she feels no one can take over at this time."

What do their sons feel about this?

"For our part, I know we still have to learn a lot of things," Paul muses, "*Pero kaya na namin siguro* (But perhaps we can now run the business)." Perhaps early exposure to the business could have minimized problems on succession.

Authoritarian Leadership Style

Both Peter and Paul feel that sometimes their mother "still tries to oversee everything."

"*Minsan nagiging personal* (sometimes it becomes personal)," Paul reflects, "Sometimes I cannot tell my mother that she is wrong because she is my mom. If it were another person, I could do it. Of course, I try to do it in a 'nicer' way—since when arguments occurs, *nagtatampo siya* (she sulks)."

"Let's just say we don't want to rock the boat," Peter adds quietly.

This trait of Nora is not lost even on her husband. "Between the two of us, I am the cool, rational-headed one, and my wife is more emotional," Jacinto offers.

"Even in the business, sometimes she shouts at some employees. I just walk away. *Ganyan lang talaga ang asawa ko. Sa totoo, malambot ang puso niya.* (That's my wife in appearances. In truth, she is soft-hearted)."

Even the boys agree.

"When Mother gets mad, she really does get mad, but it would blow over quickly. When Dad gets angry, he is silent but he doesn't forget," reflects Paul.

Nora manages most of the day-to-day affairs up to now.

"I have told her to slow down and leave more work to the boys, but she insists on being there. Of course, I know she is concerned about the business, but I want her to join me during my trips. You see, when she goes on trips, they are all businesses," complains Jacinto (nudging his wife).

Nora assents, but says she is very happy with the business and will retire only if she can be sure someone can take over. At this point, Jacinto gently chides her about "taking too much care of the boys."

He tells us, "When Peter graduated, do you know that Nora went around and tried to match-make him to all her friends' suitable daughters? And when Peter introduced us to his girlfriend, she even tried to interfere? I had to put my foot down, and tell her not to be so *pakialamera* (meddlesome)."

There is no hint of resentment on Nora's part when she hears this. She smiles and just says that she did not want her son to "marry the wrong girl," quickly adding that her two daughters-in-law are all very close to her and Jacinto.

Maternalistic Family Culture

In Dyer's (1986) terms, company culture is still paternalistic, but is actually maternalistic in the case of this family firm.

As for letting the sons take over, Nora says that she understands everybody's concern, and will let them handle more responsibilities from now on.

Individuation patterns in the Perez family and business are summarized below.

	Family	Business
Jacinto	Close to wife and children, spends time with them; may have sheltered the children too much.	Managed most of the business, mostly with wife's help, and minimal help from children; now semiretired.
Nora	Close to husband and children, spends time with them; shelters them too much up to now.	Currently manages the business with some help from children, but finds it difficult to let them take over.
Peter	Grew up sheltered, may have been overprotected by parents; now has own family but still very close to parents.	Joined the company only after graduation; not yet given responsibility for major decisions; does not want to rock the boat.
Paul	Grew up sheltered, although less so than Peter; now has own family but still very close to parents.	Joined the company only after working outside for a while; not yet given responsibility for major decisions, but is itching for it.
Prevalent style	Still enmeshed, but in the process of individuation.	Still enmeshed, but in the process of individuation.

SFI Cohesion Subscale

The parents pride themselves on family togetherness. While the sons acknowledge the closeness, they nevertheless show signs of wanting to be more independent. Their sense of togetherness is shown in the responses of Jacinto, Nora, Peter, and Paul on the Cohesion Subscale given below.

Item	Jacinto	Nora	Peter	Paul	Mean
2	1	1	1	3	1.5
15	1	1	1	1	1
19 (R)	2	1	4	3	2.5
27 (R)	1	1	1	1	1
36	2	3	2	2	2.25
Sum	7	7	9	10	8.25
Classification	Optimal	Optimal	Adequate	Adequate	Adequate

SFI Expressiveness Subscale

Although close, the Perez family is reserved as far as showing affection is concerned. Family members do not hug or touch each other. There is a clear demarcation line between children and parents. The children highly respect the parents and, in times of trouble, the children do not want "to rock the boat." This is reflected in their responses on the Expressiveness Subscale below.

Item	Jacinto	Nora	Peter	Paul	Mean
1	1	1	2	2	1.5
9	4	3	5	3	3.75
13 (R)	4	1	1	1	1.75
20	1	1	1	2	1.25
22	1	1	1	3	1.5
Sum	11	7	10	11	9.75
Classification	Adequate	Optimal	Adequate	Adequate	Adequate

The family views itself as being more cohesive rather than disengaged, a perception validated by interviews and first-hand observation.

SFI Style Subscale

Their scores for the SFI Style Subscale show that they are classified as moderate centripetal (MCP) as the Subscale below shows.

	Jacinto	Nora	Peter	Paul	Mean
Score	2.26	2.26	2.56	2.56	2.41
Classification	MCP	MCP	MCP	MCP	MCP

MCP: Moderate Centripetal

Only One Power Holder in Family and Business

Everybody in the family recognizes the power of the father in the family as well as the business. This is borne out by their answers to the interview questionnaire and my observations.

Clear Power Structure in Family

Although quiet and restrained, Jacinto is the acknowledged authority in the family. When the children were young, it was him they feared and felt answerable to when something went wrong.

"Our mother would nag but she would forget. Father would not. He would not say anything, he would just look at us, and we would feel guilty."

Jacinto and Nora were supportive of each other in raising their children. They shared in parenting but Jacinto, the father, was the one who imposed discipline.

"My wife and I discussed the rules," Jacinto explains, "and together we implemented them."

When disagreements arose, however, Jacinto's word is followed. The children apparently were not resentful, because they perceived their parents as doing this for their own good. (Paul, though, would sometimes feel they favored Peter more.) As was pointed out earlier, when one got punished, so did the others on many occasions.

Clear Power Structure in Business

As in the family, there is clear power structure in the business.

"During the lean years, when I started investing in a new machine, Nora argued with me. 'How can we afford it?' she asked," Jacinto reminisces. "I told her I had my reasons. I explained everything to her, and she consented."

What if she didn't?

"I would have gone ahead anyway and bought the machines. In hindsight, she realizes that I was right. Excellence Printers prides itself on quality, and how can you have quality if your machines are out of date?"

All through this exchange, Nora would smile and nod approvingly.

When Jacinto suffered a heart attack, the whole family prevailed on him to go into semiretirement. Was it hard for him to let go?

"Not really, because I have several other interests. As you can see, I am involved in some community work. For the most part, I am working on my recuperation. My doctor says that I should rest."

Jacinto is only semiretired, however, and not totally out of the picture. His sons report that he still "works behind the scenes." An instance involved the couple's dealings with the labor union. Jacinto took the labor strike to heart, and felt it was a personal betrayal. Bitter and quietly enraged, he had vowed to lessen the company benefits or cancel them altogether. The scholarships, for instance, used to be one for each family, but now it has been reduced to just one for the best child among all the employees' children.

"Nora may cry a lot and yell, but she has a soft heart really," Jacinto smiles.

"One time, somebody got sick and I did not want to provide hospitalization anymore. She talked me into it, and I agreed; only now it is documented."

Jacinto explains the strategy: "In business, one person has to be the good guy, the other the bad guy. I used to be the good guy. Now I am the bad guy, and my wife the good one. It seems to work so far."

Nora has taken on more responsibilities, and it is to her the sons report to daily.

"She is our immediate boss, both Peter's and mine," explains Paul. "Yet when problems arise, she still consults with our dad."

Nora confirms her sons' disclosure. As in the family, the power structure in the business is clear—there is only legitimate as well as acknowledged power holder in both spheres.

Moderate Dominance

Interestingly enough, Jacinto would like his wife to spend less time and effort working, and delegate more responsibility to the children.

"She works so hard, she gets 'hyper' sometimes," he reflects. "She can get quite emotional, and little details bother her. Sometimes, she even has to correct the grammatical errors of her secretary!"

Nora is meticulous, patient, hardworking, and desires to oversee everything, finding it difficult to delegate. Even pleasure trips overseas turn into business concerns, though Jacinto seems to indulge her in this.

"As for the secretary's errors, if I don't do it then no one will," Nora retorts. "As for the boys, I don't think they are ready to handle the business by themselves."

She insists, though, that she is slowly giving both sons more responsibility. The sons privately wish their mother would delegate more, but they admit to being trained, albeit slowly.

"Mom is definitely in the picture, but I think, if we're given more responsibilities, *kakayanin din naman ito* (we'll be able to do it)," Paul explains.

One instance is dealing with the workers. Nora already brings Peter with her to the monthly meetings, and sometimes lets him decide on how to cope with the workers' demands. Recall that leadership style in the family is authoritarian. In business, the structure is one of moderate dominance.

Individuation and Power

Individuation and power may be linked: A primarily authoritarian power structure is not always conducive to successful individuation as exemplified by this family. Did the children ever rebel when they were young? No, not really. They seem to have been, and even up to now, very obedient. Family ties are valued, and respect for parents is evident. Paul says he is bringing up his children the way he was brought up—disciplining tempered with caring.

The only difference is: "I would want them to go into the business. I am exposing them to it right now, and would like to train them, start them young."

Something which his parents regretted not having done but they, especially Nora, are trying hard to remedy.

Succession Problems

Has succession been discussed?

"Nora and I have talked about it, but not yet with the children," Jacinto reveals. "We are trying to see if they can cope together in the business. We love our sons, but we are pragmatic. They may not be capable, or they may not get along that well together. We would also be willing to break up the business into smaller ones and give one to each of them; or we could liquidate the business and divide the amount equally among them." Succession can be a problem, as a result of a non-egalitarian power structure.

Exit Style

What about exit styles (Sonnenfeld 1988)? Jacinto has the vision and brilliance of a monarch. Even upon retirement, he cannot seem to break entirely free, which classifies him as an ambassador. As for Nora, she is likely to act more as a general. Their exit styles are related to a dominant power structure.

Power relations among the Perezes are summarized below.

	Family	Business
Prevalent style	Generally led toward egalitarian leadership.	Moderate dominance toward hopefully egalitarian leadership.
Power holder	Jacinto.	Still Jacinto, though Nora holds additional power after husband's decision to semiretire.
Power bases	Legitimate, referent, expert, informational, reward, coercive.	Legitimate, referent expert, informational, reward, coercive.
Processes	Strong but quiet assertiveness; strong but silent control; generally democratic with stable leadership; husband often shared leadership with wife; somewhat flexible.	Strong but quiet assertiveness; strong but silent control; generally democratic with stable leadership; husband often shared leadership with wife; somewhat flexible.
Outcomes	Wife agrees, children obey; relative absence of conflict; good negotiation; good problem-solving; role sharing.	Wife agrees or negotiates with husband; children agree; only minor conflict; good problem-solving; role sharing.
Succession		Mixture of monarch and ambassador.

SFI Leadership Subscale

Jacinto's position as leader of both family and business is openly acknowledged by the other family members. This is shown by their responses on the Leadership Subscale below.

Item	Jacinto	Nora	Peter	Paul	Mean
8 (R)	1	1	1	1	1
16	1	1	1	1	1
32	2	1	1	2	1.5
Sum	4	3	3	4	3.5
Classification	Optimal	Optimal	Optimal	Optimal	Optimal

Fair Sibling Relations, Strong Alliance of Parents

The marital bond between Jacinto and Nora is strong while the bond between Peter and Paul is only fair. What could account for this kind of relationship between the brothers?

Strong Marital Alliances

Jacinto's and Nora's marital bond is strong and cohesive. They talk things over before making decisions, and do not contradict each other in implementing them.

Though they have different personalities, they complement each other. Jacinto is more quiet, Nora "noisier," but their team is hard to beat. One supports the other as necessary, such as during a labor problem. For once, Jacinto did not feel up to dealing with the workers, and Nora took over, doing an admirable job in the process.

The caring the couple have for each other is exemplified in this anecdote: When Jacinto was being wheeled into the intensive care unit, Nora was crying inconsolably. Jacinto had reportedly told the two boys, "*Bigyan ninyo ng tuwalya ang nanay ninyo, kasi iyak ng iyak* (Give your mother a towel, she can't stop crying)."

Jacinto is more laid back, certainly, but obviously cares for his family.

Preferential Treatment of Children

What about their treatment of the children? Both parents let on that they are equally fair to Peter and Paul. At times, however, traces of favoritism do show.

Nora cites, "*Iyan si Paul, madalas mainit ang ulo. Si Peter talagang mas mabait* (That's Paul, often hot-headed. Peter is really nicer)," her reason for not wanting Paul to deal with the workers.

Jacinto nods his approval as Nora goes on, "*Mas* good boy *si Peter* (Peter is a better boy), even in school."

Yet all this was quite subtle, and I can safely surmise that most of the time, the couple really does try not to play favorites. Even so, as we will see later, this favoritism in the family has spilled over into the business context.

Fair Sibling Relations

How do Peter and Paul feel about each other? As both of them admit, they are a lot closer to their younger brothers than to each other. They do not exactly dislike each other, "*pero madalas talaga kaming nag-aaway* (but we certainly quarrel often)," replies Paul candidly.

Even when they were young, they often ended up in fistfights, and would have to be pacified by their father.

Because of the perceived favoritism in the family, sibling relations are at times strained. Why? We see here the sibling function of differentiation at work.

Differentiation as Sibling Function

Peter, the elder one, is supposed to have more "power" than Paul, who does not see it that way. Paul wants to assert himself, and does so not by identifying with his elder sibling, but by being different from him. Apparently, both boys feel that they are relatively equal in status right now with their own families and their separate responsibilities in the company.

Aside from differentiation, perhaps this particular pattern of sibling relations turned out the way it did because Paul sensed the implicit preference of his parents for his older brother. During our private interview with the brothers, Peter appeared to be more "loyal" to his parents, contradicting Paul whenever he tried to say anything negative about them.

Let us take one instance. When asked as to whether their parents really had time for them, Paul replied wistfully that sometimes he wished his father had time to go over his homework exercises with him.

Peter counters, "You know Dad always had time for us! In fact, I remember one time when I was sick, he typed my thesis for me."

Paul makes a face and says, "*Hindi ko alam iyon a! Ang daya naman!* (I didn't know that! Unfair!)"

Paul admits, however, that generally, his parents did make time for him. He made allowances for them because he knew that they were busy with the print shop.

Thus, whatever rivalry there was simmered beneath the surface. The boys can work together (and have been doing so for quite some time), but they do not necessarily have to like each other that much.

In the office, another source of conflict between the two related to their business functions more than anything else. Recall that Peter is in charge of production and Paul of marketing. Classically, these two divisions have always been at odds, because their immediate aims vary: production stresses quality, marketing, the customer. These two factors may often be at cross purposes, no matter that the persons in charge are brothers.

"I would promise to deliver something to the client, and of course, prompt delivery is very important. Then here comes production saying that they cannot do it on time," complains Paul.

"That is because I have to make sure that the product is of good quality," retorts Peter.

How do they deal with this?

"*Nag-aaway kami* (We argue)," says Peter.

"We shout at each other," adds Paul.

Who would get the upper hand? It depends, because Nora intervenes and decides one way or the other.

Generally, though, they get along fairly well, even kid one another —well, at least halfheartedly.

For instance, when queried about future plans, Peter said, "I want to learn accounting *para hindi ako lokohin ni Paul.* (So Paul will not deceive me.)" At this, Paul pretended not to hear, and changed the topic.

In times of crises, however, both boys feel they can count on one another. Their parents have inculcated on them the importance of caring for the family, and they have always given heed. When the parents are not there anymore to intervene, however, who can predict what will happen. These instances illustrate the quality of sibling relationship in the family and the business—similarly strained and at most, fair in both contexts. Differentiation is apparent in both cases.

Succession Problems

Succession is still a problem, mainly because the brothers are not fully individuated. Moreover, because they have different temperaments—neither of which appeals to Jacinto and Nora. Peter is "too soft" to manage the company, while Paul is "too hot-headed." One plan is to break up the company into smaller ones and give each child a business of his own. Another may be to professionalize the corporation altogether. The brothers want the company for themselves, however.

"*Kung wala na sila, kakayanin din namin siguro* (When they're gone, perhaps we will be able to run it ourselves)," Paul replies. Because of their familial and business relationships, succession may be difficult.

Sibling relationships and other nuclear alliances among the Perezes are summarized below.

	Family	Business
Marital alliance	Strong, cohesive, generally consistent.	Strong, cohesive, generally consistent.
Parent-child	Close to children, but with traces of subtle alliance between Nora and Peter; no triangles.	Treatment according to child's personality; subtle alliance between Nora and Peter; no triangles.
Sibling relationships	Fair; fair negotiation and problem-solving patterns; functions: differentiation, mutual regulation, direct services; both Peter and Paul closer to the younger ones.	Fair; fair negotiation and problem-solving patterns; functions: differentiation, mutual regulation, direct services; dealing with parents (especially the mother.)

SFI Conflict Subscale

The parents perceive the conflict management of their family as excellent whereas the sons think it is critical. Note the disparity of Paul's responses from the rest especially for item number 24: "One of the adults in this family has a favorite child." The responses of Jacinto, Nora, Peter, and Paul on the Conflict Subscale are given in the following table.

Item	Jacinto	Nora	Peter	Paul	Mean
5 (R)	3	3	1	3	2.5
6	1	1	2	3	1.75
7	1	1	3	2	1.75
8 (R)	1	1	1	1	1
10 (R)	1	1	2	3	1.75
14 (R)	1	1	1	1	1
18 (R)	1	1	1	3	1.5
24 (R)	1	1	2	4	2
25 (R)	1	1	1	1	1
30 (R)	1	1	1	2	1.25
31 (R)	1	1	2	3	1.75
34	1	1	1	1	1
Sum	14	14	18	27	18.25
Classification	Optimal	Optimal	Adequate	Adequate	Adequate

Selective Acceptance of In-Laws in Business

Largely centripetal in style, the Perez family, nonetheless, welcomes outsiders especially those they deem they can relate well with. Peter and Paul each has his own set of friends, who drop in for visits.

Acceptance in Family

Although Nora wanted to pick the girl for Peter, Jacinto insisted that Peter be allowed to decide for himself.

Peter did, and married Rita, the same age as he was. Now they have two children of their own, ages 4 and 3.

Rita was accepted by her in-laws. As grandparents, they doted on their grandchildren. During a Sunday interview with Jacinto and Nora at the family home, Peter, Rita, and their children dropped in for a visit. The kids ran to make *mano* (kiss [the] hand) while Rita announced that they were going to hear Mass. This apparently gladdened the hearts of the couple. In-laws are accepted, even welcomed in the family. Business, however, is an entirely different matter.

Problems with Entry into the Business

When Rita wanted to help out in the printing business, nobody foresaw any trouble. She was assigned a comptroller position and reported directly to Nora. After a few months, though, it became clear that Rita did not have enough know-how in handling accounts.

"*Nagkagulo na* (It became chaotic)," recalls Nora. "Jacinto and I talked it over and we decided that it would be better for her to leave."

The Perez couple told Peter who asked who will break the news to his wife.

"We never mentioned it again," Nora remarks.

Rita promptly left. Were there ill feelings?

"Probably only a little," Nora shrugs. "She never showed it to us, and vice-versa. For a while, I think things were strained, but right now, she is as close to us as ever."

Peter has a different version.

"Rita understood because she was not feeling happy about her duties either. And at that time there was that labor problem. *Maraming nagpatung-patong.* (Several [things], one on top of the other.) She was glad to leave."

He added that this did not affect in any way his relationship with his parents. The Perez couple had a nice idea. They had long wanted to start a jewelry business. They asked Peter what he thought of it. Peter was agreeable and they put Rita in charge. This has proven to be a good move because Rita is running the shop to this day.

How about Paul? He married Grace, a year his junior, and they have one child, age 3. The grandparents treat him well as they do Peter's. During an interview at the plant, Paul's son was playing in Jacinto's lap. The closeness of the extended family to the old couple is plain to see.

Grace works in another firm—a cosmetics company—from Monday to Friday. On Saturdays, she trains as finance officer of Excellence Printers. She must have shown promise, for Jacinto says he wants her to take over that post someday. There is a difference between in-law entry into family and business—they are welcomed only if they are capable. Thus, conditional acceptance is the norm as far as business is concerned.

Ambiguity in Succession

As for succession, are Rita and Grace eligible?

"Excellence Printers' shares will be divided equally between Peter and Paul," Jacinto asserts. "It is up to them to apportion to their own families." As has been noted earlier, succession may be a problem.

Professionals and Other Outsiders

Although in-laws are conditionally accepted, professionals and other outsiders are mistrusted entirely. Despite this feeling, Jacinto is open to the idea of going public.

Absence of Professionals

Currently, nonfamily members are not in any decision-making position. All managerial positions are occupied by the immediate Perez family themselves. Employees make up the rank and file.

Jacinto and Nora are firm—they will not place an outsider in a "sensitive" decision-making position, not even somebody who has been working for them for years.

Mistrust of Outsiders

"You can never totally trust them," Nora remarks sadly. "Besides, they don't have the necessary expertise."

This attitude is, of course, bolstered by the labor strike which Jacinto felt as a personal affront. Redding's (1990) research on Asian companies (where company ties are perceived to be almost familial) confirms this.

As for the sons, both feel that if the company wants to expand, then they may have to hire professionals in the future. (Possibly, their parents would have retired by then.)

As of now—"This is not necessary."

Paul adds, "All major decisions will be made by the family even if professionals were hired."

Based on Davis's 1991 classification, this professional will be picked largely because of competence, and not loyalty per se. He or she will most likely be a transient. (If the family is fortunate, then the professional can be a superstar.) The mistrust of the Perez couple toward outsiders is the main reason for rejecting the entry of professionals.

Public Ownership

Interestingly, Jacinto is open to the idea of going public. Recall that he emulates San Miguel Corporation, a company listed on the exchange, yet still managed by a family. He would want Excellence Printers to go that route.

Going public may also be a Solomonic decision, should the couple be unable to decide which son, if ever, is going to succeed them. Their other plans, as we have seen, are to split the business in two and give one part each to the sons, or to sell the company altogether. Even if the Perez couple are not amenable to the entry of professionals, they are willing to go public if needed.

Family First Before Business

From the preceding discussions, we can use Beavers (1990) Interactional Scales and summarize the Perezes' family functioning as follows:

1. *Structure of the family*
   a) Overt power: Marked to moderate dominance
   b) Parental coalitions: Strong
   c) Closeness: Amorphous, vague, and indistinct boundaries among family members at times, with sons attempting to differentiate.
2. *Mythology.* Mostly congruent ("Family comes first before business.")
3. *Goal-directed negotiation.* Fair to good
4. *Autonomy*
   a) Clarity of expression: Somewhat clear
   b) Responsibility: Members sometimes voice responsibility for individual actions, but would also blame others.
   c) Permeability: Moderately open

5. *Family affect*
   a) Range of feelings: Obvious restriction of some feelings
   b) Mood and tone: Usually warm and affectionate
   c) Unresolvable conflict: Some evidence of unresolved conflict without impairment of group functioning
   d) Empathy: Generally emphatic responsiveness with one another despite obvious resistance.
6. *Global health-pathology scale.* Adequate (4)

SFI Health/Competence Subscale

The Perezes see themselves as a healthy family with the parents painting a picture more positive than that of the children Peter and Paul. This view is apparent in the responses of Jacinto, Nora, Peter, and Paul on the <u>Health/Competence Subscale</u> below.

Item	Jacinto	Nora	Peter	Paul	Mean
2	1	1	1	3	1.5
3	3	1	2	3	2.25
4	1	1	2	2	1.5
6	1	1	2	3	1.75
12	1	1	2	2	1.5
15	1	1	1	1	1
16	1	1	1	1	1
17	1	1	1	1	1
18 (R)	1	1	1	3	1.5
19 (R)	1	1	4	3	2
20	1	1	1	2	1.25
2	1	1	1	2	1.25
24 (R)	1	1	2	4	2
25 (R)	1	1	1	1	1
27 (R)	1	1	1	1	1
28	1	1	2	2	1.5
33	1	1	2	3	1.75
35	2	1	1	3	1.75
36	2	2	2	2	2
Sum	23	20	30	42	28.75
Classification	Optimal	Optimal	Adequate	Adequate	Optimal

A summary of Excellence Printers' <u>business functioning</u> according to Dyer's checklist (1986) is presented below.

1. The family is quite aware of the problems it is now facing.

2. The family is currently in the process of planning for future family and business needs.

3. A well thought-out management succession plan has not yet been made.

4. The family has not yet developed an ownership succession plan.

5. The leader and the (possible) successors (sons) are interdependent at times, but the sons have to assume more responsibilities.

6. The sons and a daughter-in-law are now undergoing training for key positions in the business.

7. Members of the firm do not share similar views on equity and competence. (Note their reactions to the strike.)

8. In general, family members work together to solve problems, though the parents still make the final decisions.

9. The family manages conflict fairly.

10. Family members generally trust each other but the trust is not extended to nonfamily employees.

11. The leaders do not have outside feedback mechanisms.

12. The family has a generally balanced perspective on family and business needs, though the mother has to try to wean herself from too much attention to the business.

The Hernandez Family: Quality Shoes

Leon and Conchita Hernandez have seven children—five boys and two girls. Conchita took care of two more children, Leon's by another woman, and treated them as her own. Following Conchita's magnanimity, the original Hernandez children treat them as their own siblings. Conchita, 69 years old, is now a widow.

I was able to interview Conchita, Chito, Susan, Tes, Atoy, and Ellen.

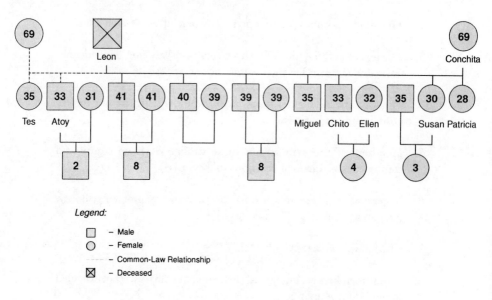

The Hernandez Family Genogram

The organizational chart of Quality Shoes still includes Leon Hernandez, its founder. Conchita, Leon's widow, is the treasurer while Tes, Leon's daughter by another woman, is assistant treasurer. Miguel, the eldest among the sons residing in the Philippines, is president and general manager. Chito acts as manager in charge of marketing and production. Atoy, Tes's brother, is assistant manager for production.

Susan, the elder daughter, is the manager in charge of retailing and purchasing.

Branch managers and the rank and file occupy the lowest rungs of Quality Shoes' organizational structure.

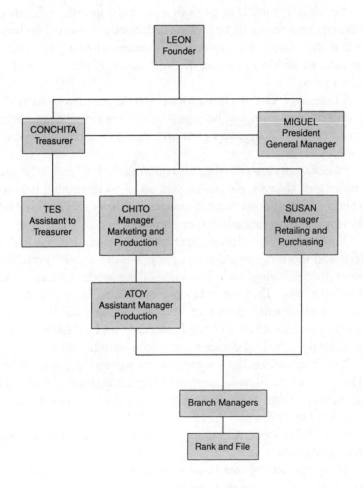

Quality Shoes Organizational Chart

"Our father started Quality Shoes in the mid-forties. He died five years ago," reminisces Miguel Hernandez, 35. "He and Mom got married when he was 25 and she was 20. They both came from Marikina, and they knew how to make shoes. They started from scratch, and did all the manual labor by themselves—sewing, making the soles, seeing to the leather. When the orders multiplied, they started hiring workers.

"Actually, I think Dad got into a partnership with someone once, but this guy backed out. So he and Mom decided to continue the business. Our first shop was in the house, and I remember, *parang* playground *sa aming lahat na mga bata iyon noon* ([it was] like a playground to all of us children then)."

There were a lot of Hernandez kids to be sure; seven all in all; five boys and the two youngest, both girls. The three elder boys were only a year or two apart in age, and grew up helping their parents in the shoe factory.

"They were close, but they also quarreled a lot," recalls Susan, 30, the older girl. "Maybe the reason why all of us remaining here are so close is because we don't want to quarrel like they did! I am only joking. They stopped bickering when they grew up."

"During our schoolyears, business really expanded. We had more orders, and more clients started coming. We put up one branch, then another, then still another. When some of our workers formed a union and called a strike, Dad wanted to give everything up. I think his manic depression was starting at around this point. So, all three of my brothers decided to take more care of the business to let Dad have a rest. Dad agreed; by then, he had decided to go into semiretirement."

The Hernandezes did not give in to the workers' demands. A branch had to close down. To make matters worse, a store burned down. Those were unhappy years compounded by Leon, the patriarch of the clan, taking on a "second wife."

How did his wife, Conchita, the mother of seven children, deal with this infidelity?

"*Iyong mga sakit ng loob ko, isinusulat ko na lang sa liham sa kanya* (My resentments, I simply wrote to him)."

Conchita did something even more heroic—she forgave him and "the other woman"—and even accepted Leon's two children by her. The children, Tes and Atoy, are as old as her own fourth and fifth sons.

How did the other children handle this situation?

"Mom treated them well so what are we her children to do? We have to treat them well, too. They are considered part of the family," Susan explains.

For a few years, the three elder sons helped in the business, but the United States beckoned. All three (in fact, every child in the Hernandez clan) took up business-related courses and decided to migrate separately. After making sure that their remaining siblings would take over the business, all three went abroad. The eldest now works for a stockbrokerage firm, the second for a computer company, and the third for a bank.

"Of course, since they can already fend for themselves, their allowances are cut off," explains Conchita with a twinkle in her eye.

"*Parang* communism, *di ba?* (Just like communism, isn't it?)" Miguel retorts. "You see, even when Dad was alive, Mom handled the payroll. In our business, everyone is given an allowance. Mom is very strict even to herself. When she wants to borrow money from the company, she gives herself a voucher, too. Everything is recorded properly."

It was then up to Miguel to take over the reins. His father was succumbing to more manic-depressive phases which eventually caused his death. His mother was not getting any younger. In childhood, he dreamed of being a pastor, but it was not to be. "*Hindi ka kasi* qualified (Because you're not qualified)," his sister Susan teases fondly.

Miguel finally realized that his calling was along another path, literally close to home. He grew up in the shoe factory, and never wanted to go into any other business.

"It was the one thing I knew how to do."

And how he did. Still a bachelor to this day, Miguel devotes full time to the business, being both president and general manager. Under his management, earnings expanded. Sales shot up 40 percent from the previous year reaching the ₱200 million mark. The company recently launched a T-shirt line which earned more than a million in the first year (but Miguel was still dissatisfied), and even shot its commercials on location in Florida.

"Our elder brother, the second son, got married last year, so all of us went to Miami, and we decided to have the company advertisement done there, too." In the next few years, they intend to establish outlets there.

Miguel has always loved challenges, and his latest one is to improve computerization of the business operations. He also wants to revive shoe lines abandoned by his brothers and his father. "We used to have this brand which I am thinking of reviving. It was very famous in the Philippines, but we stopped manufacturing it because of labor problems."

[I encouraged him to revive the brand, for I recognized it as that which my very discriminating mother used to patronize.]

Miguel would need help, and who could give it better than his brother and sister?

Chito, 33, dreamed of being a pilot, but had to abandon the dream because of imperfect eyesight. "It's okay. Right now, I handle the marketing and production end of the business." After receiving his MBA degree, Chito married his college sweetheart, a practicing ophthalmologist with her own clinic. They have a child, now 4 years old.

Susan, 30, married a dentist who also has his own clinic. After graduating with a degree in management economics, she worked for a while in the travel industry, but eventually decided to help out in the family business. Presently, she handles the retailing and purchasing end of Quality Shoes.

"I love my job. In fact, all of us slid into our positions just naturally. I mean, I could never imagine myself in production!"

The only problem facing Susan these days is her husband's wanting them to migrate to the U.S. with their 3-year-old daughter in tow. "I have to train somebody to take my place, and that is difficult to do."

"So as you can see, my sons and daughter have taken care of everything. Our youngest is still working for another firm, however, we are not forcing her into the company. She knows she is always welcome. As for me, I am semiretired now. I just go into the office and look at the payroll and distribute the checks—with a little help from Tes here. That's all!" A rejoinder from Conchita after which a chorus of yells erupts from the clan.

(Conchita insists that she spends most of her days working for church groups and doing charity work. Semiretirement seems to suit her.)

It is indeed a tribute to Conchita that she treats her "stepchildren," who live with them, with fairness and kindness. Although the major decisions are still made by Miguel, Chito, and Susan, Tes and Atoy both draw salaries, too.

Tes, 35, helps Conchita with the finances. Atoy, 33, handles the manufacturing end. He is married and has a 2-year-old son whom the clan dotes upon.

What are their plans for the future?

"We want to expand. We already have more than 10 branches in Luzon, and we recently opened one in Cebu. We are looking at a Davao branch and hopefully another one in the United States."

They have more than 200 employees and profits are increasing. In the future, Miguel plans to go public, but as it is, he is keeping his fingers crossed. The founder Leon used to dream of a school for shoemaking, but when he died, the idea was shelved. The Hernandez children hope to establish it someday.

As for succession, "we haven't discussed it yet. It has not become an issue yet."

Perhaps so, because Miguel and his siblings are still young.

He admires Ferragamo, the Italian shoe company renowned worldwide for quality and excellence.

"That is our dream—to be like Ferragamo."

The company philosophy? "Strive for quality. Work toward excellence. Take care of your family. Live and let live."

Fully Individuated Siblings

The clear division of labor and leadership, perceived fairness and discipline, and the love in the family contributed to the individuation of the family members.

Division of Labor and Leadership

There is effective division of labor in family and business. Leon is the leader in the business while Conchita's domain is in the home. Leon had been gregarious before illness struck. He would go out with his *barkada* (peer group) and have fun. When problems started hitting the company, however, he lapsed into depression. Although he would talk to his friends about possible solutions, he never broached them to his family, not even his wife. None of the children we interviewed ever recall discussing business problems over the dinner table, but at that time, they admitted that they were too involved in schoolwork to care.

Aside from working in the business, Conchita was running the household, balancing the budget, cooking the meals, and making sure the kids were doing fine in school.

Discipline and Fairness in Family

It was up to Conchita to discipline the children.

"Dad was quite soft, he would give in easily," remembers Susan. "It was Mom who spanked us but she was very fair. I remember this one rule: If one of us got spanked, all the rest also got spanked. We used to hate it, but it also made us think of other people." Discipline and fairness are practised hand in hand in the Hernandez family.

Parents' and Children's Love

"You realize I stopped spanking all of you long ago. You see, I attended this seminar in 1970 and the speaker said that spanking is not so good. Love your children *na lang* ([Just] love your children). So I did. And speaking of love, if Leon were still alive, I would still be getting roses every Valentine's Day"—this said with a twinkle in Conchita's eyes.

Conchita has earned the love and affection of her brood, that's for sure. She balances discipline with a sense of humor, and always strives to be fair.

"I have no favorites. I love my children equally. And I always tell them to play fair, and to take care of one another"—and all of them nod in agreement.

This fine balance has enabled the children to grow up with a sense of responsibility and caring for each other. They are neither too enmeshed nor too disengaged.

"When I was in high school, I remember sharing a room with my younger sister. We would meet the rest for meals and share jokes and the happenings of the day. I was closer, of course, to Miguel and Chito and Patricia because they were closer to my age. Our three eldest kuya took care of us. There were a lot of us in the house, but no one violated our privacy. We had our boundaries, yet we were pretty close," Susan reflects.

"Basically, we know when to leave each other alone," Miguel adds.

The ones who were "naughtiest" were the three eldest boys, who engaged in fistfights in the factory floor. "That's probably because they were almost the same age; you know how young boys are."

Yes, fight they certainly did, but they banded together when it counted—to protect their business and help their father. When it came to business, the three rarely quarreled among themselves.

They grew up in Marikina which was then considered boondocks. They did not go to discos or pool halls, but basically played among themselves at home or invited friends over. Conchita preferred this, too, for security's sake. All these illustrate the family members' love and concern for each other in every aspect of their lives.

Fairness in Business

Conchita's sense of fairness extends to the business, where as the one in charge of allowances, she gave each one an equal share. Does Miguel or Susan resent this? No, for remember, when they were young, everybody got punished for one child's infraction. They grew up with these rules, and for them, the regulations seemed fair.

The three eldest boys seemed the most independent of all, striking out on their own in the United States. (They keep in frequent contact with the family here; nevertheless, the whole clan flew over recently to attend the wedding of the second son.)

Susan is all set to follow their path to the United States, however, and what do the remaining relatives feel about this?

"It's okay with us," volunteers Miguel amiably. Nonetheless, Susan feels strongly about training a good substitute before leaving.

Susan may be the most assertive of the lot. During our interview, Miguel, though in command, was quiet and self-effacing. Chito rarely spoke but smiled often. It was Susan who brimmed with self-confidence and is quite streetsmart. "I was in this social service club in college, but when I graduated, I became disillusioned. Still, there are lots of nice people around."

According to her sister-in-law, Chito's wife: "Susan is strict as a mother. One time, her daughter wanted to play with mine for a while, but Susan said, 'It's time to go' and her daughter obediently went."

(I observed that Susan balances her strictness with affection. This is so perceptible seeing her daughter cuddled in her lap while she was being interviewed.)

Leon reportedly had no favorites either. He was a lot more lenient and easygoing except when he went into depressive stupors, and "we would all just avoid him." The fairness in the family also shows in the business.

Family Togetherness

What Conchita felt upon finding out that her husband "took another wife," no one really knows. (We did not probe too much because the "state of affairs" speak for themselves—her "stepchildren" are accepted and loved, and dined with us at the same table.) Susan admits that even her own children do not talk to her about it too much, and only follow her example of acceptance.

"Leon had his faults, but he was conscientious in providing for his family," Conchita quietly asserts. Family is emphasized over business—anytime.

Participative Company Culture

Dyer (1986) classifies business culture in this case as participative, with Miguel as the leader, but frequently consulting with his siblings and mother on major decisions. The participative family style also reflects on the company culture.

Succession Unresolved

What about succession? "We haven't discussed it yet. Anyway, we are still young. Life is too short for it to become an issue," offers Miguel.

The family seems to be skirting another issue, though. Like their father before them, they find it difficult to talk about sensitive topics. When business problems occur, for instance, Leon would keep mum about it even to his wife, his partner, even though they love each other and are even romantic (flowers each Valentine's Day). For another, when Leon had an affair, his wife did not talk ill of him to her children. Likewise, with succession being an uncomfortable topic, they just "don't talk about it."

Balancing Act

Seemingly, this behavioral pattern corresponds to Wynne's (1958) pseudo-mutuality. This family survived serious crises with their bonds intact and as strong as ever. Perhaps, their secret is in knowing when to pry and when to just back off.

The family is sometimes centrifugal (e.g., the father has an affair, the elder sons go off), sometimes centripetal (e.g., the father and mother are close, the elder sons keep in constant touch) in style.

Even if more communication may have been better, most psychologists believe that a healthy family should be a combination of centrifugal and centripetal, and the trick is to know when to use which method. As for each member's need for privacy, this becomes clear when we realize that there are several people under one roof, and one of the best ways to individuate is to have a private space, a place of one's own.

Although not members of the nuclear family, Tes and Atoy are nevertheless treated as such especially by Conchita. Atoy is married and has a child, and seems to be in good terms with Chito.

I feel, however, that Tes is very attached to her stepmother, both in the home and in the business. In fact, she is Conchita's personal assistant. During the interview, she said virtually nothing, and only nodded when a question was directed at her. She sat beside Conchita, and would put food on her plate from time to time—with great care (not that Conchita needed to be served, she looked hale and hearty and fit). Tes' SFI scores shows that she identifies with this family, and is in good terms with them.

As a whole though, the Hernandezes have successfully individuated, as is obvious from their family and business relationships. Their individuation patterns are summarized below.

	Family	Business
Leon	Generally close to wife but some emotional cutoff during sickness; close enough to children but lets wife take charge of them.	Welcomed wife into business after marriage, had joint and separate responsibilities; trained children and let them handle business after he got sick; now deceased.
Conchita	Close to husband; functional adaptation (welcomed stepchildren, loved husband even after he hurt her); balanced discipline and trust with children and stepchildren; let them grow on their own; maybe too close to Tes, maybe too enmeshed with her.	Made own decisions, but also consulted with husband; took care of finances; fair in business matters; allowed children to take responsibility; now semiretired, has Tes for personal assistant.
Miguel	Closer to mother than father but individuated well, has own family but still close to mother and siblings and stepsiblings.	Now heads business; makes decisions but often only after consultation with mother and siblings.
Chito	Closer to mother than father but individuated well, has own family but still close to mother and siblings and stepsiblings.	Makes decisions in his division but still consults with Miguel and others.
Susan	Closer to mother than father but individuated well; has own family but still close to mother and siblings and stepsiblings.	Makes decisions in her division but still consults with Miguel and others.
Tes	Very close to stepmother; may not be fully individuated; close to siblings and stepsiblings.	Assistant to Conchita; consults with stepmother in making decisions.
Atoy	Close to sibling and stepfamily; individuated well; has own family.	Assistant to Chito; consults with stepmother in making decisions.
Prevalent style	Individuated.	Individuated.

SFI Cohesion Subscale

The responses of Conchita, Miguel, Chito, Susan, Tes, and Atoy on the Cohesion Subscale are recorded below.

Item	Conchita	Miguel	Chito	Susan	Tes	Atoy	Mean
2	1	2	1	3	1	2	1.67
15	2	2	1	3	1	2	1.83
19 (R)	3	2	2	2	1	1	1.83
27 (R)	2	1	1	2	1	1	1.33
36	2	3	2	3	1	3	2.33
Sum	10	10	7	13	5	9	9
Classification	Adequate	Adequate	Adequate	Midrange	Optimal	Adequate	Adequate

Tes seems to want to present a terribly positive view of the family by giving the highest scores possible. This may be the Hawthorne effect, or a sign that she has not yet individuated fully. [4]

SFI Expressiveness Subscale

Interestingly, Tes once more gave the highest possible ratings on the Expressiveness Subscale. She may have wanted to please her stepmother by doing so, or she may really have felt welcomed by the clan. Susan is slightly more critical, but she still considers her family adequate. Their Expressiveness scores are given in the table below.

Item	Conchita	Miguel	Chito	Susan	Tes	Atoy	Mean
1	1	1	2	2	1	2	1.5
9	3	2	2	3	1	1	2
13 (R)	1	1	1	1	1	1	1
20	1	1	1	3	1	1	1.3
22	1	1	1	3	1	1	1.3
Sum	7	6	7	12	5	7	7.2
Classification	Optimal	Optimal	Optimal	Adequate	Optimal	Optimal	Optimal

---

4. The Hawthorne effect results when the subject or the one tested is conscious that he or she is being observed or tested.

SFI Style Subscale

As for style, the males give slightly higher ratings, indicating a more mixed style. Again, keep in mind that for Filipinos, these scores may well be considered mixed rather than purely centripetal. Their Style scores are given below.

	Conchita	Miguel	Chito	Susan	Tes	Atoy	Mean
	2.04	2.26	2.34	2.26	2.12	2.26	2.21
Classification	MCP	MCP	MCP	MCP	MCP	MCP	MCP

MCP: Moderate Centripetal

Clear Division of Power Then and Now

There was and up to now a clear division of power in the family and in the business. Consequently, the transitions in the family as well as in the business have gone smoothly.

Division of Power

When the children were growing up, Conchita was the power in the family. Leon was busy with the business, and it was entirely up to her to discipline and raise the brood.

"Our father was quite soft, and he would give in to everything we asked for," Susan recalls. "Our mother was the one we were scared of when we got low grades."

This power, apparently, was exercised fairly; all the children attest to that. Conchita never played favorites—a feat, given the number of children she had to raise.

What about the relationship between the couple themselves?

Conchita reminisces, "Division of labor was very clear. Leon was in charge of the business, and I was in charge of the family. This happened even when I was handling the business. You see, Leon handled more of the business so I had more time with the children. It was something we agreed upon."

Consequently, when it came to raising the children, Conchita had virtually a free hand. Leon never quarreled or argued with his wife about the kids; he supported her in that aspect.

When Leon began having his episodes of depression, Conchita had to be even stronger. Aside from the household and some business responsibilities, she had to take care of a husband as well. She apparently balanced everything, and in the process earned the love and respect of her children and stepchildren.

One interesting behavioral observation was the following: During the interview, Conchita would "talk for" some of the children especially Tes and Atoy, and would even interrupt Susan or Miguel. Whenever this happened, the child being interrupted would respectfully stop and let Conchita speak her mind. Conchita, however, did it gracefully without putting snags in the flow of the interview. After the interruption, her words would be acknowledged, almost always agreed with, and taken into consideration the next time the issue came up.

Did the children ever disobey their mother? None of them could remember any of that ever happening.

"Of course there were the usual teenage rebellions, I think," Miguel frowns. "I don't remember anymore. Come to think of it, I don't think there was any major incident worth mentioning or else I would have remembered."

Susan and Chito agree.

"I think we were just lucky. We were never into drugs or late nights and all that stuff. We did quite well in school. The worst things that happened concerned the three eldest boys. Sometimes they would fight each other—you know how boys are. Our mother would get mad and spank them. I think that was about it." The foregoing accounts confirm the clear division of power in both the family and business areas.

Individuation and Power

The clear delineation of power between the mother and the father as well as fairness in imposing discipline result in individuated persons as the Perez children exemplify. How did they all turn out to be such "model" people?

"I don't really know," Susan says, "maybe it's the environment. We did not live in the city so we were not exposed to vice like beer or bars. Although basically, it could be because we respected our mother. Her life and her actions became the model for all of us especially the way she welcomed Tes and Atoy."

Clearly, example shown rather than coercion is a stronger influence on behavior. Conchita practices what she preaches in the family as well as in the business.

"Our mother is very fair as well in her position as treasurer. Sometimes, we would just want to get something from the coffer, you know, for personal stuff. We inadvertently found out that she accounts for her own withdrawals, too, her own expenses, so we felt ashamed. It follows that we cannot just get money without proper accounting, either."

When her husband was alive, Conchita admits that he made most of the major decisions. Responsibilities were gradually transferred to her and the three eldest sons who have a consensual style of decision-making.

("I let my sons do most of the work, however, I want to retire already. There are so many things I want to do like help in civic groups and parish clubs.") The relationship between individuation and power is striking. A participative power structure seems to have contributed, in the case of the Perez family, to successful individuation.

Smooth Transitions

When Leon died and the three sons went abroad, the power was accorded to Miguel, the eldest who is still in the Philippines.

"It was very natural because Miguel was the oldest among those who stayed here, and he already had some experience working with our elder brothers. Nobody questioned his authority." It is clear that one positive side effect of an egalitarian power structure is smooth transitions between generations.

Egalitarian Leadership Style

Miguel asserts that power in the business is mostly shared among themselves.

"Each one of us has his own turf, and we rarely step on each other's toes. We are all satisfied with what we do because we all know everybody profits when we do our best."

Decision-making is by consensus. "We meet first thing Monday mornings, mostly to report on the happenings during the past week. We seldom argue. When an issue arises, we all talk it over and usually reach a decision which everyone is happy about. *Hindi naman pormal na pormal itong* process (This is not really [a] formal process), but everyone gets to talk."

Succession seems to be the only issue this remarkable family has studiously avoided. When pressed for an answer, they still could not come up with a satisfactory reply. Apparently, no one has ever brought up the topic, possibly because everybody is still young, and plans are afoot for expansion and not for succession per se.

"Whatever we do, we are decided on one thing. Shares will be divided equally among all family members working in the business. And if the business gets really huge, then we can spin off the company into smaller ones and everyone gets his or her section. Fairness is the most important consideration."

Family members include the stepsiblings. (None of the in-laws are in the business so in-laws become a moot issue.) These instances are simply reiterations of the egalitarian structure of the Hernandez family.

With his vision and dedication to the business, Leon displayed signs of the monarch. The three elder sons, with their short terms of office, and having broken away completely from the firm, acted more like governors. With his openness, flexibility, and penchant for shared decision making, Miguel may finally exit in ambassadorial style. Their exit styles are reflections of their egalitarian leadership stance.

Power relations among the Hernandezes are summarized below.

	Family	Business
Prevalent	Egalitarian.	Egalitarian.
Power holder	Conchita.	Leon, then three eldest sons, now Miguel.
Bases	Legitimate, referent, reward, coercive.	For all: legitimate, expert, reward.
Processes	Strong assertiveness and control, fairness, flexible leadership.	For all: moderate assertiveness and control, shared and flexible leadership.
Outcomes	Love and respect of husband and children; some acting out by husband; good problem-solving and negotiation; rules followed.	Good problem-solving and negotiation; smooth transfer of power; respect by family; rules normally agreed upon.
Succession		For Leon: monarch; for three eldest sons: governor; for Miguel: ambassador.

SFI Leadership Subscale

The children are all grown up now, and control their own lives. The power, which Conchita wielded before, is now only minimal as the need for it is gone. The children are the respective power holders in their own families, but what is remarkable is the closeness, respect, and esteem they hold for one another up to this day. The responses of

Conchita, Miguel, Chito, Susan, Tes, and Atoy on the Leadership Subscale are summarized thus:

Item	Conchita	Miguel	Chito	Susan	Tes	Atoy	Mean
8 (R)	1	1	2	2	1	2	1.5
16	1	2	1	3	3	1	1.8
32	3	2	3	2	3	4	2.8
Sum	5	5	6	7	7	7	6.2
Classification	Adequate	Adequate	Adequate	Adequate	Adequate	Adequate	Adequate

Good Sibling Relations with Equal Powers

The children of Conchita and Leon feel that they were treated fairly by them. They are respected and loved by the children. As a result, sibling relationships are good and the children cooperate in family matters. They perceive the business as theirs.

Good Marital Alliance

In general, the marital alliance between Leon and Conchita was all right. They loved each other and romance was still there even way past middle age. Division of labor between them was clear: Leon had the business and Conchita the home. The marital alliance, albeit imperfect, had enough love going for it.

How do we explain Leon's taking "a second wife?" This is the wild card here, and I did not want to explore it too much, because the situation cannot be better than it is right now. Miguel and Susan would evade it whenever I asked but answered obliquely by assenting that both Tes and Atoy are beloved members like the rest of the family. No mention was made of "the other wife." Susan believes that her father did it because he was "already starting to get sick—manic-depressive" and at the same time "the business was going through tough times." (Recall that a store burned down, a strike was staged, another store closed.)

To her children, Conchita was the acknowledged power in the home, as was later validated by Miguel and Susan.

"Our father was softer, so we would go to him if we wanted something. Sometimes we would succeed, although when our mother would hear about it, she would interfere, and he would yield to her."

Consistent and Fair Treatment of Children

The children did not succeed in pitting one parent against the other, and soon stopped trying. Just the same, all of them agree, "Our parents treated us equally."

No mean feat, indeed, for a brood of seven. There are no triangles here. This fairness extended to the business and is so up to this day.

As the treasurer, Conchita was "so fair that she would give each of us, including herself, the same amount of allowance," Susan marvels. "How could we not treat each other fairly? Our mother set the example." The fairness practised in the family shows in the business.

Excellent Sibling Relationships

Among the seven children, Miguel admits that the three eldest boys were the closest because of age (1 year apart from each other). They would play together, fight one another, shout at each other. Inspite of this, they did not neglect the younger ones (Miguel is 4 years younger than the third) though the roles were different.

"They took care of us since they were the kuya." The siblings enjoy excellent relationships among themselves.

Legitimate Power Structure

We can safely conclude that the three eldest wielded more influence over their younger siblings, but this power was considered legitimate and is based on expertise, experience, and age. When the business started having problems, all the three eldest banded together and helped their father.

Obviously, they did a good job. Business was resuscitated, transfer of power was smooth. By then, Miguel had joined the company, and he was also being trained. Chito and Susan followed suit later on. With the three eldest so close to each other, did the younger ones form alliances of their own? Susan and Miguel are not sure.

"We are all close to each other," Susan remarks. "I think I am slightly closer to Patricia, our youngest, because she is also a girl. We can talk about female stuff, you know."

Miguel agrees, saying that he tended to talk to Chito more than anybody else. These partnerships are in any case very fluid and flexible, and they do not prevent the others from joining.

"Basically, we heeded our mother's advice to take care of each other. And we do. We really care for one another."

The mantle of company president has fallen on Miguel's shoulders, a responsibility he readily takes on. The others find this state of affairs perfectly natural because Miguel was the next eldest, had the most training, and was perceived by the three eldest siblings and Conchita, especially, to be the successor. With an egalitarian power structure, it comes as no surprise that legitimacy operates in both family and business.

Diffusion of Power

Chito and Susan see themselves as equal, but with a clear division of labor. This division is an outgrowth of their different interests.

Susan puts it thus, "Chito is in production and I am in retailing and that's just fine with both of us. *Mas hilig ko ang* (I am more inclined to) purchasing. I can never see myself in production!"

Fortunate, indeed. Anyhow, have the siblings ever argued?

"Of course we do sometimes; but minor, only. We hold a family business meeting in the office every Monday morning. We talk things out then come to a consensus. Normally, *wala namang gulo* (no trouble) because we have separate areas of responsibility."

They have different strengths, and as a result, they complement rather than contradict each other. This includes the stepchildren, Tes and Atoy, who each have their own duties and spheres of influence.

Do the stepsiblings feel left out of the "original circle"? There seems to be no indication of this. During the interview, everyone seemed to be in good terms with each other with Atoy chatting with Chito, Tes with Conchita. Atoy's son was there, and was fussed over by his grandmother, uncles, and aunts. Tes did not say much, but appeared comfortable enough. We can see here that this diffusion of power in the business stems from a similar situation in the family.

Succession Unresolved

Do they foresee problems with succession?

Miguel is emphatic. "No, we will divide the shares equally among those who are working." This undoubtedly includes Tes and Atoy.

As for the three sons abroad, they do not receive allowances anymore because "they already have their own businesses," says Conchita. "We don't have to help support them anymore."

If and when Susan leaves, the same will happen to her. They are individuated enough with their own families to raise. It is a fair-enough arrangement for everyone.

Sibling relationships and other nuclear family alliances are tabulated below.

	Family	Business
Marital alliance	Generally all right, consistent.	Strong, consistent.
Parent-child	Generally equal treatment, perceived as fair; no triangles.	Treatment perceived as fair, based on age and expertise; uniform training, no triangles.
Sibling relationships	Close alliance among three eldest sons; slight alliance between Susan and Patricia, between Miguel and Chito; good conflict management; empathy; functions: direct services, mutual regulation.	Close; division of labor according to expertise and interest; good conflict management; Miguel, the acknowledged authority (based on age and expertise); functions: direct services, mutual regulation; slight alliance between Chito and Atoy (same division).

SFI Conflict Subscale

The perceptions of Tes and Atoy do not seem to differ from those held by the others. Susan is the most critical (recall that she acted quite streetsmartly), but her response is well within the adequate range. Four siblings, throw in two more—it's certainly remarkable how they can hurdle conflict and still remain close to each other personally as well as professionally. The answers of Conchita, Miguel, Chito, Susan, Tes, and Atoy on the Conflict Subscale are given below.

Item	Conchita	Miguel	Chito	Susan	Tes	Atoy	Mean
5 (R)	3	2	1	2	3	1	2
6	1	1	1	2	1	2	1.3
7	2	1	1	1	2	1	1.3
8 (R)	1	1	2	2	1	2	1.5
10 (R)	1	1	1	1	1	1	1
14 (R)	1	1	1	1	1	1	1
18 (R)	3	1	2	3	1	1	1.8
24 (R)	1	1	1	2	3	1	1.5
25 (R)	2	1	1	2	1	1	1.3
30 (R)	3	1	2	1	2	2	1.7
31 (R)	3	2	2	3	2	2	2.3
34	1	1	2	3	2	2	2
Sum	22	14	17	23	20	17	18.8
Classification	Adequate	Optimal	Optimal	Adequate	Adequate	Optimal	Adequate

In-laws in the Business

Although in-laws are readily accepted in the family, they have to be trained first if they want to join Quality Shoes. They will also receive their share when the business is divided equally among those who are working in the business.

Acceptance into Family

We have seen how the stepchildren were accepted into the Hernandez family without apparent repercussions. Individuated yet close, is it any wonder that in the family in-laws are loved as well?

During our interview, the entire nuclear family, together with their respective spouses and children, was there—a loving clan palpably affectionate with one another.

Acceptance into Business

Miguel is still single, but if he marries, "My wife will have a choice on whether or not to join us. I plan to do the same with my children. They will be exposed to the business, but not forced into it. I want them to experience what we went through."

Susan is married to a dentist who has his own clinic. The couple plans to leave for abroad with their daughter.

"No, he never thought of joining Quality Shoes," she laughs.

Would they accept him if he did?

"Maybe, but he has to be trained first."

Chito's wife is an ophthalmologist, who has her own clinic, too. She never thought of joining the company, but if she did, she would be just as welcome.

Patricia has not yet joined Quality Shoes. She is still in school. The youngest, she has no intention of getting married yet.

Atoy's wife works in a bank and does not plan to join the family business. If she did, though, she would probably be treated the same way Susan's husband and Chito's wife are.

Tes is still single, and sticks close to Conchita. On the whole, the in-laws are welcomed and loved—both in the family and in the business.

Eligible Successors

As we have noted, the issue of succession has not been thoroughly discussed but Miguel insists that the company will be divided equally among all those working there—the founder's children and stepchildren. By implication, in-laws are excluded, unless they plan to work in the company, too.

Only Family Members In

The Hernandezes think that only family members can fill top management positions. The lower-ranked positions, however, are open to outsiders.

Absence of Professionals

"As you can see, we are a big clan," laughs Susan. "We don't really need professionals to help us."

Indeed. Mother, children, stepchildren, perhaps even in-laws, in the near future—nobody feels the need to let outsiders into the business. Currently, only family members are in senior management. The highest positions that hired professionals hold are those of branch managers. All other outside employees comprise the rank and file. The main criterion for hiring? Competence. In Davis's (1991) terms, the hirees would either be superstars or transients.

"At this point, we would rather keep Quality Shoes to ourselves. Because, really, our parents built it. I think that is understandable enough," Miguel explains.

The employer-employee relationship is sufficiently fair. There used to be labor problems during Leon's time, but currently "things are a lot more stable. In fact, we are thinking of expanding."

Would they get outside help to expand?

"Only for the labor. We will still do the major decisions. We can manage by ourselves," says Miguel. We can surmise that the family can afford not to hire outsiders because they perceive themselves sufficient for expansion purposes.

Public Ownership

The family is, nonetheless, open to the idea of going public. That move would give them more capital, but again, the family will retain a controlling interest. Management, of course, would be the exclusive domain of the Hernandezes. (Band [1992], calls this sort of board a statutory or caretaker one.) We can see that even if professionals are not needed in the management of the company, they may be welcome in the financial aspect.

Looking After Each Other

Using Beavers Interactional Scales, let us summarize the Hernandez family functioning.

1. *Structure of the family*
   a) Overt power: Egalitarian
   b) Parental coalitions: Moderate
   c) Closeness: Close with distinct boundaries among members

2. *Mythology.* Mostly congruent ("Family members should look after each other.")

3. *Goal-directed negotiation.* Good

4. *Autonomy*
   a) Clarity of expression: Clear
   b) Responsibility: Members are regularly able to voice responsibility for individual actions
   c) Permeability: Receptive

5. *Family affect*
   a) Range of feelings: Some restriction in the discussion of some topics (e.g., concrete succession issues)
   b) Mood and tone: Generally warm, affectionate, humorous, optimistic
   c) Unresolvable conflict: Little unresolvable conflict
   d) Empathy: Consistent empathic responsiveness

6. *Global health-pathology scale.* High adequate (3)

The Hernandez family members are satisfied with relationships among themselves. Susan is slightly more critical, but she still feels the family is sufficiently healthy as a whole. The table below lists the responses of Conchita, Miguel, Chito, Susan, Tes, and Atoy on the <u>Health/ Competence Subscale.</u>

Item	Conchita	Miguel	Chito	Susan	Tes	Atoy	Mean
2	1	2	1	3	1	2	1.7
3	2	1	1	2	1	1	1.3
4	1	1	1	2	2	1	1.3
6	1	1	1	2	1	2	1.3
12	2	1	1	2	1	1	1.3
15	2	2	1	3	1	2	1.8
16	1	2	1	3	3	1	1.8
17	1	1	1	2	1	1	1.2
18 (R)	3	1	2	3	1	1	1.8
19 (R)	3	2	2	2	1	1	1.8
20	1	1	1	3	1	1	1.3
21	1	1	1	3	1	1	1.3
24 (R)	1	1	1	2	3	1	1.5
25 (R)	2	1	1	2	1	1	1.3
27 (R)	2	1	1	2	1	1	1.3
28	1	1	1	3	1	1	1.3
33	2	1	1	3	1	2	1.7
35	2	1	2	2	1	2	1.7
36	2	3	3	2	1	3	2.3
Sum	31	25	24	46	24	26	29.3
Classification	Adequate	Optimal	Optimal	Adequate	Optimal	Optimal	Adequate

For <u>business functioning</u>, Quality Shoes can be rated adequate, after summarizing the detailed rating following Dyer's (1986) checklist:

1. The family generally seems aware of some problems it may face in the future, although it tends to skirt sensitive topics like succession.

2. The family has talked about future needs, but no definite plans have been made.

3. So far, there has been no well thought-out management succession plan, but no problems are anticipated on that score.

4. The family wants to divide business ownership equally among members working in the company, but has not formalized its intent.

5. The leader (Miguel) and his possible successors work independently.

6. Future leaders are currently being trained.

7. Members of the firm generally share similar views on equity and competence.

8. Family members collaborate in solving problems.

9. The family manages conflict situations well.

10. Family members trust each other very highly. They have a good working relationship with employees, who are, however, not as well trusted as family members.

11. No outside feedback mechanisms are in place.

12. The family has a balanced perspective concerning family and business needs.

The Gochiamco Family: Gochiamco Groceries, Inc.

The Gochiamco family is headed by Tirso, 69 years old, who is married to Grace, 65 years old. They have four children: Boy, age 41; Caloy, age 40; Bosco, age 39; and Rosa, the only girl, age 34. They are all married.

Boy has a 9-year-old son. Caloy has two sons, ages 8 and 6. Bosco has two children, a son, age 9, and a daughter, age 7. Rosa has a daughter, age 5.

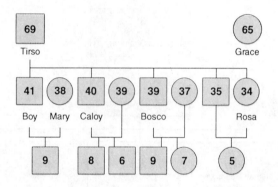

Legend:

▢ – Male
◯ – Female

The Gochiamco Family Genogram

The president and chairman of the board of Gochiamco Groceries, Incorporated is Tirso Gochiamco. Grace, its founder, is vice-president and board vice-chairperson.

Their three sons head the three departments of the family firm. Boy heads the human resources department; Caloy heads, although in title only, property and maintenance; Bosco heads operations. All three are members of the board.

In the same rank as the brothers, as far as the organizational chart is concerned, are Mary and Rosa. Mary, the wife of Boy, "sits in the board" but has no voting powers. Rosa, the only girl and the youngest of the Gochiamco siblings, is member of the board.

Below the board members are the senior managers who are professionals. Next come the middle managers composed of branch managers; then the junior managers who are division managers.

Occupying the lowest positions in the hierarchy are the rank and file. Like the senior, middle, and junior managers, they are all considered outsiders by the Gochiamcos.

I was able to interview four—Tirso, Grace, Bosco, and Boy.

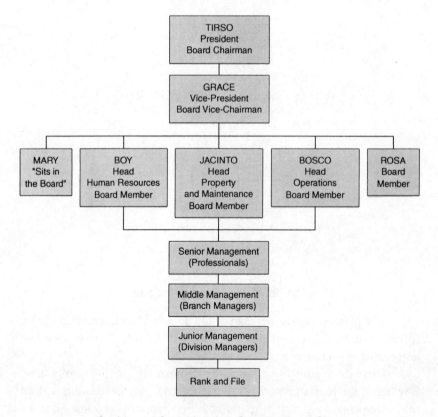

Gochiamco Groceries, Inc. Organizational Chart

It was Grace, the vice-president, who started it all. Growing up during the war years, the young lass from Sorsogon was highly independent. Her family owned some *sari-sari* (variety) stores, and she helped out during weekends and summer vacations.

Their business grew, but after her parents' death, her many siblings argued about the division of the spoils. There were heated altercations and everybody started taking what they could. Relationships were so much broken that up to this day, many refuse to talk to one another. Personally witnessing how money could mess up family lives, Grace promised herself that it would not happen with her own.

Grace traveled to Metro Manila for college, staying at a house her parents bought and furnished for this purpose. She finished with a psychology degree, which she never practiced.

Marriage beckoned right after graduation, and keeping house with Tirso, a bright, up-and-coming lawyer, was tantalizing. He is "one-fourth Chinese" who can barely speak the language and whose grandfather was a prominent philanthropist in the local Chinese community. They settled in the city, and four children did come—Boy, Caloy, Bosco, and the only girl, Rosa—but with Tirso going off to the law office early in the day and coming home late in the afternoon, Grace wanted to "have something more to do."

In 1955, using part of the inheritance from her parents, Grace opened her first sari-sari store. It was in the house she was living in at the outskirts of the city when she was in college.

"Actually, I spent virtually nothing on the place because it was already ours. With a ₱5,000 loan from a bank, we were ready to start."

The grocery area was on the ground floor with private quarters on the second level.

"At first, there were very few customers. The first couple of years were difficult. Tirso was beginning to protest because I could not attend social functions with him. I persevered because I do not believe in stopping something just because it is difficult. If I start something, I finish it."

Hard work paid off. The sari-sari store slowly expanded with the floor area widened at all corners, the second floor transformed into a warehouse, and a third level added. Grace started out doing almost everything herself (buying merchandise, selling to customers, accounting, and so on), with the household help pitching in part-time. With expansion, she started hiring full-time personnel, but she worked alongside them, often 16 hours a day, seven days a week.

By this time, her sons were growing up, and Grace required them to help out during breaks much as she herself did so many years ago. Sometimes the boys grumbled, preferring to play basketball rather than count change. They did help anyway because they were disciplined and respected their parents. All of them, without fail, did very well in school—a premier exclusive boys' school in Metro Manila. Everything seemed to be going fine with the Gochiamcos.

During this time, too, Tirso was becoming well-known as a fair and intelligent lawyer. Believing in the community spirit, he immersed himself in the Lions Guild, the Rotary Club, and eventually became a congressman. Following in his father's footsteps, he became widely known as a philanthropist.

"If you ask around in our town, there is no church or foundation which approached us for money that got turned away."

Unlike his wife and her family, Tirso is still very close to his siblings. They take care of each other and get together regularly. His father was a talented entrepreneur and gave all his children a comfortable inheritance, but Tirso himself admits, "I am a lawyer. I am not much of an entrepreneur. It is my wife who is the businessman [sic] in our family."

Still, Tirso's analytical skills, influence, and reputation have proven to be valuable assets, and it is only natural that he enter the grocery business, too. It is a tribute to the couple's love for each other and Grace's respect for her husband that Tirso was made president of Gochiamco Groceries, Inc. in 1976, while she retained the position of vice-president.

All the children were given equal shares in the company—even if eventually some would not work there. The couple did not force any of them to run the grocery business although the rewards were plainly visible.

The eldest, Boy, now 41, stayed in law school for two years but did not like the atmosphere. Later he would confide that it was his dad who wanted him to follow in his path. Still, with honors from college and a political science degree tucked under his belt, Boy was able to land interesting jobs, one being a member of a senator's staff. His father's civic-mindedness evidently rubbed off on him.

Boy managed people very well, and it was he, together with Tirso, who mediated in union problems. Some workers were demanding "more pay and less work," but the Gochiamcos were firm and sent this ultimatum: Either get your separation pay right now or wait until the company goes bankrupt.

The union leaders silently filed past the office and got their pay, and never bothered the company again. There are no unions right now, but there is a cooperative, manned by store managers and key employees, which approves loans, negotiates bonuses, and so forth.

The cooperative, of course, is Boy's idea. Everybody acknowledges his human resources skills, and it comes as no surprise that he was made head of the human resources division of the burgeoning grocery enterprise.

Married with three children, Boy also "allowed" his wife Mary to be involved in the business, to some extent. She sits in on monthly board meetings, but has no shares and cannot vote.

"She doesn't really say much. *Siya ang nakikibagay sa pamilya* (She gets along with the family) and not the other way around," reflects Bosco, the youngest brother.

Does this bother Mary? No, because she has her own franchising business to take care of.

This state of affairs brings us to Caloy, 40, the middle brother. Running his own electronics concern, Caloy rarely spends time and effort in the family grocery business. He sits in during board meetings, but mostly "he would just sign checks." Technically, he holds the position of head of property development and maintenance, but this is just a title, and the bulk of his work—taking care of assets and maintaining them—rests mostly on Bosco. His wife does not involve herself either, and instead helps her husband in their electronics business. They have a son.

Bosco, 39, the youngest brother, is head of operations in every way. With a management degree and graduating with honors, Bosco has put his education to good use. He reads up on finances, marketing, cost-cutting, and streamlining operations, and stocks up on business books. Right after college in 1980, he went into the grocery business and never regretted it. He taught business courses intermittently, only on a part-time basis.

With him and Boy at the helm, business expanded. Branches started opening in the 1980s, one after the other, up to date. The Gochiamcos can boast of nine stores. Ever since Bosco came in, assets have increased more than 200 percent and employees more than 250 percent. With around 40 workers in each branch from the manager on down to the rank and file, this would bring the number of employees to 250.

Desiring their business to be made as professional as possible, the brothers conducted training seminars themselves, invited their father to give motivational talks, or even some "priest friends to discuss morality." Turnover rate is low, possibly around 3 per 250 every year.

By his own admission, however, "my brother is more the people person, while I am of the administrative mold." For instance, Bosco tried negotiating with the union but soon lost his patience. He told them, "If you want, buy us out and give us the salary instead." Thankfully, Boy intervened and steered the negotiations toward a more positive tone.

Bosco, though, is the de-facto chief operating officer. He handles most of the day-to-day operations and works overtime in the business. His father is retired and his mother, semiretired. He is married with a son and a daughter, but his wife has her own shop and does not involve herself with Gochiamco Groceries, Inc.

Rosa, 34, the youngest, is married and is living in Britain. She does not concern herself with the business, but has shares equal to her brothers'.

Gochiamco Groceries, Inc. has made a name for itself in the grocery industry in the country. They are among the top 20 in the industry. Bosco is not satisfied, however; he wants to expand even more all over the country, and in the future, perhaps even abroad. Talks are ongoing with six other grocery owners to put up a giant warehouse-type store patterned after similar concerns in the United States.

At present, all store managers are professionals but the board is still composed of kin members. The family is not closed to the idea of letting outsiders in, but "maybe someday, if we plan to go public." Bosco is quick to add, though, that the family should retain 60 percent of the shares, "the public can get 40 percent." Controlling interest stays within the family.

Treating their employees well is a prime concern. Across the board salaries are higher—₱200 a day as compared to ₱120 given by other grocery firms. Bonuses are given whenever somebody gives birth; and of course, sick leave is mandatory. The Gochiamcos plan to improve the cooperative setup, possibly with profit-sharing and commissions. Tirso would also like to establish a foundation in their name and everybody agrees this may just come true.

From his study of family corporations, Bosco realizes that succession may be a thorny issue. Even if all his brothers are still healthy, he is already thinking about it at this point. He is firm about one thing, though: everybody gets equal shares (though not equal salaries) regardless of the input to the company. It is the next generation which worries him—he has several nephews and nieces and coupled with his own children, division of spoils may be more difficult.

"I am thinking that far ahead," he volunteers.

What does he envision the company to become? Walmart.

"Sam Walton was able to expand his business ingeniously and divide the inheritance among his children nicely. He also treated his employees very well."

For Grace and Tirso, their ideal company is a local one run by a mestizo friend.

"It is very successful, and Don is such a nice person. He is trustworthy and fair and treats his employees decently."

What guides this extraordinary family?

"Work hard. Help others. Play fair. Do not forget family and God."

Individuated Siblings Close to Parents

The Gochiamco children have successfully individuated as the following interview results and observations show.

Balancing Act

Remarkably, all the children in this case have grown into self-confident and independent adults who still maintain close ties with their parents. How did this come about?

It's a matter of correct upbringing. Parenting was a husband-wife issue with responsibilities shared between Tirso and Grace.

"Early on, we taught the boys to rely on themselves and on each other. For example, I remember once when Bosco was small. He fell and extended his arms for me to pick him up. He wasn't really hurt so I told him to get up by himself," Grace reminisces.

How did Bosco feel about that?

"I have to admit—it was tough. Also, during the first day of school, when my mother just left me there—while my classmates' parents stood outside waiting for them—I felt a sense of loss. But I quickly realized that I had to learn to fend for myself, and now I am thankful for the training they gave me. It made me what I am now." Here, we can see the balance between holding on and letting go which the Gochiamcos successfully did.

Parents with Own Identity

"What makes it easier to understand is my parents often taught by example. They themselves were very independent. They had their own interests yet they were always there for each other. They treated us the same way. During troubled times, we ran to them and they guided us." We can surmise that parents with their own interests find it easier to make room for the children to grow.

Fairness and Discipline in Family

Their mother tutored them in the first two grades even if she had a lot of other things to do.

"When I saw they could do assignments on their own, I slowly left them alone."

The children have a nursemaid (yaya) and maids, but they were taught to pack their own bags and bring them to school. Self-reliance was instilled early on.

Both parents were "very fair." Once, when the young Bosco and Boy had a fight, Bosco went to his father and complained about how the elder one "bullied him." Instead of favoring Bosco and scolding Boy, Tirso just listened and then called Boy to hear out his side. He then talked to both boys together and they made up.

Another illustration: Once, the youngest, Rosa, snatched a doll from her cousin who was older than she. The father of this cousin told Tirso that it was okay because his own daughter should have shared the doll with the younger girl. "Nevertheless, I made Rosa give the doll back and apologize," Tirso remembers. "She had to learn to do the right thing."

Comparing his parents, Bosco feels that his father used to be "the strong silent type with his sons, although he was gregarious with his organizations. Mother was more verbal and would be the one to really scold and nag us. (Looking back now, I am more like my mom in temperament, and Boy is more like my dad. He keeps his cool while sometimes I scream.)"

He and his siblings were more scared of their father because "sometimes, he would just look at us and we would feel guilty. Don't take me wrong—we all felt very secure with him. We know he loves us."

Discipline was enforced though not rigidly.

"If the children did something wrong, *pinapadapa namin at pinapalo* (We make them lie on their stomach then spank [them].) I would give them two spankings each with all my might so they would not forget and repeat the same mistakes," Tirso reflects. "We never spanked on the first offense—only *kung inuulit* (when repeated)."

This seemed to have been effective because after the spankings, the children "never made the same mistakes; if they did, at least it was very seldom."

Education was important and both parents impressed on the children that schooling was necessary. Watching television was not allowed during the week (a practice all their children continued with their own family now). Nobody ever complained because they were all brought up that way.

"*Nasanay na sila* (They're used to it)." That Bosco would later concur.

"The trick is to start them young. They are easier to mold then or else you would have problems later on," Grace reflects.

They excelled in class, never went into drugs, never violated curfews. Up to this day, they still automatically address their parents by *po* and *opo*, their dad and mom "Papa" and "Mama," never by their first names.

"They were nonetheless allowed to speak their minds," Tirso hastens to add, "but only if they showed respect."

"They see this with us," Grace affirms. "Even if we are angry at them, we never scold them in front of our people. We show respect for them as persons." These revealing anecdotes show that the Gochiamcos practice what they preach: fairness and discipline in the family as well as in the business later on.

Early Exposure to Business

During summer vacations, all four children were expected to help in the grocery store. Boy was especially unhappy at this because "he wanted to play basketball with his friends." One time, he confided to Bosco, "We work so hard in school yet we still have to work during summer and Christmas." Bosco admitted he felt the same way, but neither ever complained to the parents.

Why not?

"Because we saw how hard they worked," Bosco says sheepishly. "We knew that training in the store was for our own good, but you know how kids are. Eventually, we stopped grumbling and started liking it. I always knew I would join the business and because of my training, my parents trusted me to handle it the moment I joined."

He was right.

"I was able to trust my children because when they worked there during breaks, I saw how they handled money. They are intelligent, and *hindi naman gasta nang gasta* (not just spending [and spending])," Grace muses. Evidently, one factor which led the children to be capable in the business is their early exposure to it.

Individuation Achieved

"Bosco was able to prove to us that he was capable of managing the business. He was very good with finances—dealing with income statements, making sure profits went up, that inventory did not pile up. I guess that was part of his training. So we gave him minimal supervision. Would you believe that only a year after Bosco joined the company, Grace and I took a trip abroad and told our sons, Bosco and Boy, to run the business on their own?" Tirso chuckles.

"I knew they would be scared, but we had confidence in them," he continues.

"We were only in our early twenties at that time and we loved the freedom to make our decisions," Bosco reflects. "Except as luck would have it, problems started cropping up the moment my parents left. What did Boy and I do? We called up some good friends of our parents—also in the grocery business—and asked for their help. They were able to make *salo* (save; literally, catch). When Papa and Mama got back, everything was fine."

(Sonnenfeld [1988] would term Grace's and Tirso's departure "ambassadorial" without the negative connotations.) These instances only serve to drive home one point that individuation has been successful in this family.

Family Togetherness

Even though the parents were busy with the business and the children were in school during the week, Sunday was family day. The Gochiamcos went swimming the whole day and came back in time for an excellent supper. In this way, family togetherness was affirmed regularly.

Tirso got this sense of family from his own. "I admire my father-side relatives. There are a lot of them, but they are very close to each other to this day. They love to go to family gatherings and call each other up to check up on things," muses Bosco. "I think my father took after them. He always said that if it comes to that, he would readily sacrifice business for his family. I feel the same way, too."

The contrast with his maternal relatives is evident.

"I know my mother feels bad about what happened with her side of the family; that's why she always tells us to take care of each other. She doesn't want the same thing to happen (to us)."

Division of labor in the company suits everybody just fine. Bosco puts in the most time and effort, but his shares are equal to his three siblings'.

"No, I don't resent it. Papa and Mama kept telling us when we were young that we should take care of one another and that the business belongs to the whole family, not just to them." We can see here that family concerns are emphasized over everything else.

Participative Company Culture

Company culture is participative (Dyer 1986) in Gochiamco Groceries, Inc. and the succession issue is being addressed this early. Bosco would like to train his children the way he was trained by his parents because "it is really effective." He stresses, though, that he would make sure that "it would be seen more as play, at least, since they are all still so young." It comes as no surprise that the business reflects this trend because the culture in the family is egalitarian.

Fairness in Business

Bosco will not force them into the business, but he hopes his children will show an interest. Whatever the case, shares will be divided among all of them (all his siblings' children) equally.

Apparently, the sense of fairness the parents tried so hard to imbue in their children has been instilled successfully. The fairness in the family is also felt in the business.

Parents' and Children's Love for Each Other

Now grown up, they feel grateful to their parents for their upbringing. I feel that this sentiment can best be described by one of the children. In a letter to Tirso last year, Boy wrote:

> As I grow older, time seems to go by faster. Each year is shorter than the previous year, today more fleeting than yesterday.
>
> Nowadays, I feel a deep urge to say the things which are important to me while the opportunity remains.
>
> At 40, I am old. My physical powers have begun diminishing. The strength is still there but the endurance, speed and agility are slowly fading away.
>
> Thank God for the spirit, intellect, and wisdom. Age is no barrier to creation as far as these three elements are concerned. The world still lies at our feet waiting as we ponder on whether to live in divine harmony with it or refashion it in man's image.
>
> I wonder how you must feel. Whatever moods you have, I believe that the underlying and everlasting feeling you have must be one of gladness, great accomplishment, and satisfaction in a life well-lived.
>
> In an observation borne by long study and stripped of personal bias, I find that you are one of the greatest creatures that ever walked on this earth. You have already succeeded in entering the Holy Dimension, a place denied to us plain mortals while we tread on this earth.
>
> It was my most blessed luck to have been born your son.
>
> Happy Father's Day!

Individuation patterns in the Gochiamco family and business are summarized below.

	Family	Business
Tirso	Very independent himself, so trained children to be self-reliant early on; shared parenting duties with wife; has own interests, but close to wife.	Helped wife in business, but has own profession; trained children early on and let them handle business on their own; now retired.
Grace	Very independent herself, so trained children to be self-reliant early on; parenting duties shared with husband; has own interests, but close to husband.	Supported husband in his career but has own business (which husband has helped in); trained children early on and let them handle business on their own; now semiretired.
Boy	Individuated; has own family and interests, yet still close to parents and siblings.	Manages his own division, but consults with Bosco on major decisions.
Caloy	Individuated; has own family and interests, yet still close to parents and siblings.	Has own shop; has a title in the business but normally leaves management to Bosco; retains company shares equal to everybody else's.
Bosco	Individuated; has own family and interests, yet still close to parents and siblings.	Manages most operations, but consults with Boy on major decisions.
Rosa	Individuated; has own family and interests, yet still close to parents and siblings.	Has own business abroad, but retains company shares equal to everybody else's.
Prevalent style	Individuated.	Individuated.

SFI Cohesion Subscale

The Gochiamco family views itself as close yet independent. This is reflected in the Cohesion Subscale below.

Item	Tirso	Grace	Boy	Bosco	Mean
2	1	3	3	2	1.75
15	1	1	1	1	1
19 (R)	1	3	2	2	2
27 (R)	1	1	2	1	1.25
36 (R)	1	1	3	3	2
Sum	5	9	11	9	8.5
Classification	Optimal	Adequate	Adequate	Adequate	Adequate

SFI Expressiveness Subscale

On expressiveness, both parents feel that they have given the children enough freedom to express themselves, a sentiment the two boys generally agree with. The family's Expressiveness scores are shown below.

Item	Tirso	Grace	Boy	Bosco	Mean
1	1	1	1	1	1
9	1	1	2	3	1.75
13 (R)	1	1	2	3	1.75
20	1	1	1	1	1
22	1	1	1	1	1
Sum	5	5	7	9	6.5
Classification	Optimal	Optimal	Optimal	Adequate	Optimal

SFI Style Subscale

Keeping the Filipino and Chinese cultures in mind, these scores shown in the table indicate that family members view themselves as being balanced—they feel that they have mastered the fine art of togetherness and independence. The congruence between the scores of the parents and children for Style is remarkable.

The family's responses are recorded below.

	Tirso	Grace	Boy	Bosco	Mean
	2.26	2.56	2.04	2.56	2.35
Classification	MCP	MCP	MCP	MCP	MCP

MCP: Moderate Centripetal

Clear and Legitimate Power

In the Gochiamco family, the power structure is clear in both the family and business. The leadership style is egalitarian and succession, as a result is not a problem.

Clear Power Structure in Family

Tirso is the acknowledged authority figure in the family, the one who makes the decisions. This responsibility he generally shares with his wife, who says "he seldom finds a need to contradict me since I tend to see his point, and he always has a good reason behind every demand."

In making major decisions, the partners would talk it over such as when Grace wanted to start a business on her own. Though sometimes worried that she could not attend social functions with him, Tirso generally supported her. She, in turn, shared the task of raising the children with her husband.

They were consistent and quite fair in enforcing discipline. Although the sons might privately grumble at the achievements expected of them, they admit that their parents are excellent role models. Power was not arbitrarily imposed. When rules were given, they were explained to the children who generally were obedient.

Tirso's sense of justice is shown even outside the family to the community at large. The following illustrative anecdote confirms this quality.

When he was congressman, a son of his friend was arrested for selling shabu. Tirso called up the chief of police and asked for the details of the whole thing. Upon determining that the boy was really guilty, "with a heavy heart, he told the chief to do his duty."

Justice is tempered by compassion. Once, an errant tricycle driver got scared when he realized it was a congressman's car he accidentally hit. Tirso's own driver assured the man saying, "*Huwag kang matakot kasi hindi magagalit si Sir. Alam niyang hindi mo sinasadya* (Do not be scared because Sir will not get mad. He knows you did not mean to do it)."

Were the children scared of their father?

"Sometimes," admits Bosco, "when we knew we did something wrong."

Punishment was not imposed indiscriminately, however.

"Papa would never take sides. Sometimes, when I would complain to him about Boy or Caloy, he would just listen to me, then call either one and likewise listen to them. He would then talk to all of us together."

What about their mother?

"She supports Dad in everything. We are sometimes scared of her, too." The power holder in the family is clear and legitimate.

Clear Power Structure in Business

In business, though, the one who used to have the final say was Grace because she is the founder and the more expert one. Tirso even admits that his wife is "more of a businessman *[sic]* than I am." As in the family, the power holder in the business is clear and legitimate.

Egalitarian Leadership Style

When the children began taking over, the bulk of decision making was left to them. Authority is divided between him and Boy, insists Bosco.

Who wields more power?

By all accounts, Bosco handles most of the operations.

"So sometimes, if it is just a minor matter and Boy is not there, I decide. But I always tell the family about it later."

They respect each other's authority, nonetheless.

"Boy has his division and I have mine. We are the authorities in our respective areas."

Do they have arguments? Certainly. Who wins?

"It depends. We listen to each other and try to reach a decision satisfactory to both of us. We normally are able to do that."

How can they have such smooth relations?

"We owe our caring for each other to our parents. They always told us family comes first before anything else, certainly not business. We would not sacrifice our personal relationships for the sake of profits. So, we end up sharing authority." The leadership patterns in the business reflect those in the family.

Succession Not a Problem

Succession is not a thorny issue because the transfer of power from the first to the second generation has been done effectively. Tirso and Grace were able to let go more easily because they trusted their children and because they each had outside interests.

"I am busier now than I used to be," Tirso laughs. "I am currently involved in this project of giving awards to outstanding mothers and policemen."

For her part, Grace welcomes semiretirement. She can spend more time with her husband and also with her own set of friends. Because of their family and business relationships, succession is not a problem.

Exit Style

Their exit styles (Sonnenfeld 1988)?

With her emphasis on the capability of her successors ensuring a smooth transfer of command, Grace is an ambassador; and with his broad outside interests and minimal involvement in the business per se, Tirso is the governor.

As for the succession to the third generation, "We are currently thinking about it," Bosco says. Hopefully, it will be as smooth.

Most probably, like his mother, Bosco will exit as an ambassador. Boy, like his father, will most likely be another governor. Their exit styles reflect their egalitarian leadership modes.

The <u>power relations</u> in the Gochiamco family are presented in the table below.

	Family	Business
Prevalent style	Egalitarian.	Egalitarian.
Power holder	Tirso.	Grace, then Bosco and Boy.
Bases	Legitimate, referent, expert, informational, reward, coercive.	Legitimate, referent, expert, informational, reward, coercive.
Processes	Moderate assertiveness, strong control, shared and flexible leadership.	For Grace: strong assertiveness and control, flexible leadership. For Bosco and Boy: moderate moderate assertiveness and control, shared and flexible leadership.
Outcomes	Love and respect by wife and children; obedience by children; good negotiation and problem-solving; role sharing; rules normally enforced.	For Grace: respect by husband and children; smooth transfer of power; rules generally enforced; good problem-solving. For Bosco and Boy: good negotiation and problem-solving, role sharing, respect of employees.
Succession		For Grace: ambassador. For Tirso: governor. For Boy: governor. For Bosco: ambassador.

SFI Leadership Subscale

Tirso is evidently the leader of the family, with his legitimate authority accepted by all. Yet he exercises power judiciously, with fairness and justice. Now, with the children grown up, wielding of power is minimal. The responses of Tirso, Grace, Boy, and Bosco on the Leadership Subscale are presented in the table below.

Item	Tirso	Grace	Boy	Bosco	Mean
8 (R)	1	1	1	1	1
16	3	1	1	2	1.7
32	1	1	4	2	2
Sum	5	3	6	5	4.8
Classification	Adequate	Optimal	Adequate	Adequate	Optimal

Excellent Relationships and Alliances

The Gochiamco children have excellent sibling relationships resulting from their parents' strong marital alliance, as well as the consistent and fair treatment of them. The children see each other's strong and weak points and are able to settle matters amicably.

Strong Marital Alliance

We have seen that the marital alliance between Tirso and Grace is strong. Although the acknowledged leader, Tirso seeks Grace's advice and talks things over with her before making major decisions. Because she admires his expertise and sense of fairness, things stay calm.

Consistent and Fair Treatment of Children

United in their decisions, they strived to treat their children equally. Their efforts did not go unappreciated, apparently, for Bosco and Boy affirmed later on that they could never get their parents to side with one or the other. Tattling on each other would not work. Discipline was enforced equitably. Reportedly, no dysfunctional triangles or alliances ever disturbed the functioning of the Gochiamco family.

Grace admits that often she feels closest to Rosa because "naturally, I am the mother and she is my only daughter. Besides, she is the youngest and sometimes the baby of the family." (We can see Adler's [1928] theory of enthronement at work here.) The sons do not resent this because they also dote on their sister.

Rosa, nevertheless, was also meted punishment when needed, and "in no way did my closeness with my daughter interfere or cut into my love for the rest."

The anecdote in the preceding section about Rosa and her cousin fighting over a doll is proof enough. These all illustrate the sense of fairness pervading the family life.

Sibling Relations from Childhood

How about sibling relationships?

"We were all expected to do well in school," Bosco said. "Nobody was excused from homework."

Apparently, everyone excelled in his or her own way. Boy graduated from political science and later followed his father into law practice. Caloy majored in engineering, Bosco and Rosa, in business management.

Were there rivalries among them?

"As young boys, we would sometimes have those *tampuhan* (ill humor among us), you know," reminisces Bosco. "They would soon blow over." Because neither parent would side with anyone, the combatants would be mollified and tempers would soon cool down. (Bosco does not recall any arguments with his sister.)

They were all close to their parents. While growing up, Boy discussed law with his father, and Bosco discussed the family history, wanting to learn more about his roots. He admired his father-side relatives very much and loved to listen to genealogical accounts of them.

Although the eldest, Boy was not necessarily the "most powerful" sibling.

"As far as I can recall," remembers Bosco, "we all felt we were equal to each other." Sibling relationships are excellent, from childhood to the present, in family and business.

Sibling Functions in Home and Office

The brothers served as sounding boards for each other and with their different personalities, they complemented one another. Aside from mutual regulation, the brothers alternately helped each other with homework or commiserated with one another while working in the store during the hot summer months. These experiences forged a strong bond. Because their parents displayed such strong ties to each other, the children had to balance this off by being close to one another, too.

Boy is more of an extrovert while Bosco is more of the quiet type. The eldest is gregarious, loves dealing with people, and "maybe that's why he became a lawyer!" Bosco is "better at technical things, loves to delve into operations and details of things." Caloy seems to be a mixture of both. We can see that the sibling functions are similar in both contexts—at home and in the office.

Diffusion of Power

These differences surfaced when the children went into the business. Boy naturally gravitated into human resources, Bosco into the overseeing of daily operations. With Caloy blazing his own path, division of labor between the eldest and the youngest boy had to be implemented.

Sometimes there had to be adjustments. When there was a labor problem, Bosco could not negotiate with the workers. Boy had to hastily take over, negotiate with the workers, and offer to have a cooperative established.

"I have learned my lesson. From now on, I will let Boy deal with them," Bosco smiles.

Then there was the problem of employees' uniforms. Bosco wanted everyone to wear uniforms because "customers have to know who they are, they should be able to identify the employees, and besides, wearing uniforms presents a good image."

Boy felt otherwise; uniforms should not be mandatory because "people have to express their unique personality."

The brothers had to discuss it and though the employees eventually had to wear them, Bosco was able to convince Boy to "see it his way."

However, Bosco did not always win. Once, the two decided to talk about establishing another branch. An altercation ensued and things got so heated "we had our worst quarrel ever. We did not talk to each other for two weeks."

What happened? Boy's wife Mary intervened.

"She called me up and requested me to patch things up with Boy," Bosco ruefully admits. "I did and we made it; but in this case, Boy's plans prevailed."

How did Bosco feel about this?

"It was okay because I soon saw the soundness of Boy's reasoning. He had his point. After that quarrel, we began to learn more about how the other functions, and from that time on, we had no arguments about that issue anymore." Clearly, decision making is participative.

They were a good team, so much so that Grace trusted them enough to virtually leave the business in their hands. What about inheritance and succession?

Problem-Free Succession

The obvious successors are Bosco and Boy, of course, whose training since childhood has prepared them admirably for those roles.

Shares are divided equally among all the children including Rosa abroad even if Bosco "does most of the work." He does not mind this because "for us, family is the most important. My father also says that we should take care of our brothers and sister."

Salaries, though, differ according to the effort put in. No problems on that score as everybody involved perceives the differences as being only "just."

What about the generation after theirs? "We plan to divide the shares equally, too, but as to the exact details, we haven't reached that far yet." However that may turn out, succession does not seem to be a problem.

Sibling relations and other nuclear family alliances are shown below.

	Family	Business
Marital alliance	Strong, cohesive, consistent.	Strong, cohesive, consistent.
Parent-child	Equal treatment; closeness between Grace and Rosa but no triangles.	Equal training; fair treatment; no triangles.
Sibling relations	Close; no alliances; good conflict management; empathy; functions: mutual regulation, direct services, balancing.	Close; decision-making by consensus between Boy and Bosco; good conflict management; functions: mutual regulation; direct services; division of labor among siblings; sibling with appropriate qualification deals with employees with particular problems.

SFI Conflict Subscale

Family relationships among the Gochiamcos are functioning healthily and conflicts are dealt with effectively as shown by the responses of Tirso, Grace, Boy, and Bosco on the Conflict Subscale below.

Item	Tirso	Grace	Boy	Bosco	Mean
5 (R)	1	1	2	1	1.25
6	3	1	1	1	1.5
7	2	1	1	1	1.25
8 (R)	1	1	1	1	1
10 (R)	1	1	1	1	1
14 (R)	1	1	1	1	1
18 (R)	1	1	1	1	1
24 (R)	1	1	3	1	1.5
25 (R)	1	1	1	1	1
30 (R)	1	1	1	1	1
31 (R)	1	3	1	1	1.5
34	1	1	1	1	1
Sum	15	14	15	12	14
Classification	Optimal	Optimal	Optimal	Optimal	Optimal

Exclusion of In-Laws from the Business

In-laws are welcomed into the Gochiamco family but business is another matter as their responses below show.

Acceptance into Family

The Gochiamco children are married and their spouses are all accepted and treated with love and fairness by Tirso and Grace.

"I treat all my daughters-in-law fairly," Grace asserts. "The same way I treat their husbands, our sons. Sometimes, some of them may tend to be 'aggressive' and may say the wrong thing and others may feel hurt. But I never correct them in front of others. I just talk with them privately. We have maintained our relationships, and we trust each other."

Grace states that she never interferes when her sons and their wives quarrel.

"That is their own business. Also, nobody's perfect. I see my sons' shortcomings, I see their wives' mistakes, but I don't tell anybody about them, not even my husband. That is not my place."

For his part, Tirso says he "gets along extremely well" with his in-laws. His sons have chosen well. In-laws are welcomed into the family, that's clear to see.

Partial Acceptance into Business

Boy is married to Mary who has a business of her own. By the consent of the others, Boy "allowed" Mary to "sit in on board meetings," but "this is in name only." Mary does not hold shares and cannot vote. She does not mind, though, for she has interests and a business of her own. (According to Tirso and Grace, Mary receives a salary from occasional purchasing duties on behalf of the company, but they do not want to give her a share.) As far as business is concerned, the family would rather keep in-laws out. Cultural norms are at work here.

In-law as Referee

Still, Mary is close to Bosco, and was the "bridge" between the two brothers when they quarreled.

"She was the one who called me up and requested me to make up with Boy," Bosco remembers. "We did and we are both grateful to Mary for that."

(In this case, we can see that far from being a catalyst for conflict, an in-law can actually enhance sibling relationships because she grew up apart from the "emotionality" inherent in them. Recall Mancuso and Shulman's remarks [1991].)

Caloy is also married, and his wife helps him run their own electronics business. Because Caloy rarely involves himself in the groceries business, his wife does not participate either. Reportedly, she has never expressed a desire to join.

Even Bosco, who virtually runs the business, says that his wife is not part of it either, and he would rather that she stay out. Why?

For one, he has seen how relatives can ruin the business, as illustrated by the wrangling and rivalry among his mother-side relatives, for instance. For another, well, his reasoning can be illustrated by a Chinese parable.

"My father used to tell us," Bosco narrates, "about these three brothers who vowed to be faithful and never fight each other. When their wives heard them boasting about how much they loved each other, they concocted a plan. That night, each wife whispered something to her husband. The next day, the three brothers were up in arms against each other. Fortunately, the wives calmed them down and explained everything just to prove a point: that sometimes marriage can really get in the way of blood ties."

So far, there have been no problems with Mary because "she is very understanding and efficient and does not cause any trouble at all. *Siya ang nakikibagay sa amin* (She is the one who gets along with us)."

Bosco then corrects himself saying that they are not "that closed" to having in-laws in the business but if these would prove to be *"magulo, e di huwag na lang* (chaotic, then [do] not [involve in-laws] anymore)."

Presently, his wife and Caloy's wife do not feel any deep interest to join Gochiamco Groceries, Inc. so the issue is moot. As for Rosa and her husband, they are both abroad and have a life of their own; the chances of their joining the company are slim. (Recall that Rosa has a share equal to her brothers'.) The foregoing illustrates the role of an in-law as referee even if the in-law is not really "in" the business.

Ineligible Successors

Are in-laws eligible to be board members? The Gochiamcos would rather reserve the seats for themselves.

Limiting Professionals and Other Outsiders

In spite of the presence of professionals, all major decisions are made by the Gochiamcos. As with professionals, nonfamily members are kept up to a certain level only. Because this is clear, the relationship is one of trust between, on the one hand, the owners, and on the other, the professionals and other outsiders.

Professionals for Expansion Purposes

All branch managers are professionals, a requirement because the Gochiamcos lack manpower. These managers have their own division managers, who in turn, have support staff. All of them are considered outsiders.

The company even has four professionals in senior management, three of whom are women ("during my mother's tenure, she would prefer to hire women because she felt she could trust them more especially with accounts and finances").

How much decision-making responsibilities do they have?

Enough, for the branch managers do report to them. Of course, all four still have to report to Bosco and Boy.

"The major decisions are still made by my brother and I," reports Bosco and they do not think that this situation will change soon.

"They may be in senior management positions but we are still the top managers. There are enough of us to make the major decisions," Bosco opines. "We welcome outsiders, yes, but only up to a certain level."

Apparently, outsiders can hope to go as high as senior management but can never have a place on the board. They can manage somewhat, but the owners will have the major say in the operations.

Trust and Respect for Founder

Do the senior managers resent the fact that they cannot make major decisions for the company?

"Oh no, in fact, they have been with us for years, and they know what to expect. We have a good working relationship" (reminiscent of what Davis [1991] calls "superstars").

As we have noted, Bosco and Boy pride themselves on dealing with their employees well. They even went as far as giving them personal seminars on various topics, providing training, and paying them above minimum wage. There were labor problems in the past, but they are now resolved. A cooperative (Boy's idea) was established, and has proven to be quite effective. As a result, workers tend to be satisfied, and turnover is low. The foregoing accounts clearly show that trust exists between the founder and the professionals.

Public Ownership

Does the company intend to go public?

"Perhaps, someday, but we should still have control, maybe 60 to 40 (percent). [Bond, 1992 terms this a rubber stamp board.] But that is far off. We still have enough capital to expand and set up partnerships with others. But of course, we are not closed to the idea. We have realized that one good way to grow is to be listed on the exchange." Because professionals are in the business, it is no wonder that the family is very open to the idea of going public.

Relationships with professionals and other nonfamily members are summarized below.

Professionals	Four professionals in senior management but major decisions still made by top management (Boy and Bosco); some professionals in middle management (branch managers), each with their own junior management team (division managers) and support staff; no outsiders in the board.
Public ownership	Family open to the idea of going public (for expansion purposes) as long as it retains control.
Other options	Establish more branches so younger generation can manage one each; no plans of selling company.

Fairness in Family and Business

From the preceding discussions, we can use Beavers Interactional Scales and summarize the Gochiamco family functioning as follows.

1. *Structure of the family*
   a) Overt power: Egalitarian
   b) Parental coalitions: Strong
   c) Closeness: Close with distinct boundaries among members

2. *Family mythology*. Generally congruent ("Family members should be treated fairly even in business.")

3. *Goal-directed negotiation*. Good

4. *Autonomy*
   a) Clarity of expression: Generally clear
   b) Responsibility: Members take individual responsibility for own actions, seldom blame others
   c) Permeability: Receptive

5. *Family affect*
   Range of feelings: Direct and indirect expression of many feelings (utilizing several media including writing letters)

6. *Global health-pathology scale*. Optimal (2)

The Gochiamcos all agree that their family functions healthily and competently, as shown by the responses of Tirso, Grace, Boy, and Bosco on the SFI Health/Competence Subscale.

Item	Tirso	Grace	Boy	Bosco	Mean
2	1	1	2	2	1.75
3	1	1	1	2	1.25
4	1	2	1	2	1.5
6	3	1	1	1	1.5
12	1	1	1	1	1
15	1	1	1	1	1
16	3	1	1	2	1.75
17	1	1	1	1	1
18 (R)	1	1	1	1	1
19 (R)	1	3	2	2	2
20	1	1	1	1	1
21	1	1	1	1	1
24 (R)	1	1	3	1	1.5
25 (R)	1	1	1	1	1
27 (R)	1	1	2	1	1.25
28	1	1	1	1	1
33	1	1	2	1	1.25
35	1	1	1	1	1
36	1	1	3	3	2
Sum	23	22	27	26	24.5
Classification	Optimal	Optimal	Optimal	Optimal	Optimal

The overall rating of the <u>business functioning</u> of Gochiamco Groceries, Inc. following Dyer's (1986) checklist is optimal. The outline of the assessment is as follows:

1. The family is aware of the problems and tradeoffs it is now facing and will probably face in the future.

2. The family has made some plans for future needs.

3. Management succession is ongoing according to the plans of the first generation.

4. Ownership succession is also ongoing according to the plans of the first generation.

5. The leaders and their successors have an interdependent relationship.

6. The successors have been trained, and are now taking over. As for future leaders, some training programs are in place.

7. Members of the firm generally share similar views on equity and competence (after a fruitful labor-management discussion).

8. Family members collaborate with each other to solve problems.

9. Family members generally manage conflict effectively.

10. Family members trust each other and, to a lesser extent, their employees. Working relationships, nevertheless, are fine.

11. Though there are professionals in the company, outside feedback mechanisms such as management seminars and management books are still lacking.

12. The family has a balanced perspective toward family and business needs.

The Chua Family: Snackfood Delights

There are only three in the Chua family, owner of Snackfood Delights—Emilio, the patriarch; Cecile, his wife; and their only child and daughter Helen. There could have been another child but Cecile had a miscarriage.

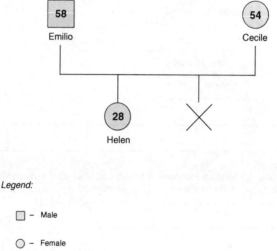

Legend:

☐ – Male

◯ – Female

✕ – Miscarriage

The Chua Family Genogram

The organizational chart of Snackfood Delights shows Emilio Chua at the head as president and chairman of the board. Immediately below him is Japanese national Hiroto San, vice-president and vice-chairman of the board.

Below them are Paeng Gapuz, finance manager and board treasurer; Tito Gomez, production manager; Helen, the only child of the Chuas, marketing manager; and Cecile, Emilio's wife, member of the board. Paeng and Tito are both professionals and outsiders, i.e., nonfamily members.

My interviewees are the three Chuas—Emilio, Cecile, and Helen; and two nonfamily members—Paeng Gapuz and Tito Gomez.

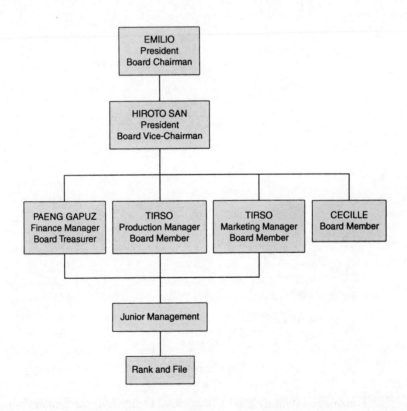

Snackfood Delights Organizational Chart

Emilio Chua comes from a well-to-do trading clan in Cebu, but he had always wanted to set up his own manufacturing concern. Aware that Filipinos love to snack, he tried his luck in the food business in the early 1960s.

His gamble paid off. He went into partnership with the son of his parents' best friends, a genteel couple from Narita Prefecture in Japan. Their son Hiroto was close enough to Emilio to help out. With his parents' help, Emilio put up 70 percent of the initial investment, and Hiroto the rest (30 percent). They built their plant in Malabon, hired workers, and soon went into business.

Hiroto was based in Japan, and was more "the silent partner." He would fly over only for meetings with Emilio once every three months on the average. He was satisfied with his investment, and trusted his partner.

Emilio managed most of the day-to-day operations. From the start, he believed in professionalizing the business. His wife was busy selling insurance, and by mutual consent, she did not help out in the business. They have only one child, Helen, whom he adored and protected as much as he could, and she was still in school.

"I really had no choice," Emilio says now. "I knew I had to get outside help. I guess I have been lucky in my choice of people. They are all trustworthy and have been with me through tough times."

Emilio was the general manager then, and he appointed three outsiders to managerial positions: Paeng Gapuz to finance, Tito Gomez to production, and Eugenio Perez to marketing.

The employees were treated well, bonuses were given based on performance, outings sponsored, parties given during birthdays, weddings, and baptisms. Turnover rate was low. There was never any problem with labor.

In 1990, Eugenio Perez told Emilio that he had to migrate to the United States with his wife. After a big *despedida*, Emilio appointed his daughter Helen to fill the position of marketing manager. Helen had been exposed to the business since childhood; she graduated cum laude in business management; she even had an MBA from Stanford; and it had been her earnest desire to help her father.

In a span of 30 years, with an initial crew of 30 employees (from maintenance personnel to engineers to managers), Snackfood Delights grew to more than 300 employees. Factory area has tripled, sales have shot up more than 250 percent, and their products have become household names in the country. The stockholders have expanded to include Emilio, Cecile, Helen, Hiroto, and Paeng. In the mid-1980s, Snackfood Delights started computerizing their accounts and updating their machines, in an effort to stay ahead of the competition.

What does the future hold?

"I intend to make this company even more competitive. We are at the dawn of a new century. We have to learn to adapt to the times," Emilio forecasts.

How about succession? Professionalization may be the key here (in Dyer's terms, company culture in Snackfood Delights is classified as professional).

"Helen is going to be part of our company, but she cannot handle it alone. We already have a team of trusted people in place, and they have the expertise and experience."

What company does he emulate? Jollibee.

"I admire the franchise concept, and I am trying to see how I can fit it into my business. Plans are still hazy, but Hiroto and I have been meeting about this. Jollibee is way ahead of the giant McDonald's hamburger chain in the Philippines, so it shows that you don't have to be Western to be at the top. It's like David beating Goliath. I find this personally satisfying. Also, Jollibee has expanded abroad. I would like to take Snackfood Delights along the same track. Hiroto says Japan is a potential market and we are exploring the possibilities."

What is the company philosophy?

"Learn about your target market and cater to them. The customer is always right. Keep ahead of new developments. Never be afraid to ask the help of others for you can never stop learning."

Enmeshment as Impediment

Emilio and Cecile love each other and in turn love (dote upon is more like it) Helen, their only child. Too enmeshed a family, it has created a problem in the business on the part of Helen who tries to individuate.

Enmeshment in Family

The Chuas are a tightly-knit family. Emilio and Cecile married at a young age, he at 23 and she at 19. They had been classmates since high school, and were childhood sweethearts in Cebu. The match was welcomed by in-laws on both sides and no one objected to their youthful union.

"In fact, my mother kept on asking why I wasn't married yet," Cecile laughs gently. "And I was only 16 then. I guess in our time, the girls had to get married early, and she was quite worried why Emilio had not yet proposed." It is easy to see that the family is very tightly knit, maybe too much so.

Parents' Love for Each Other

After the wedding, the couple came over to Manila to make their home. After a few years, they were blessed with Helen, which added to their joy. But then Cecile miscarried after, and the doctors had to remove her uterus, which meant she could never have children again. For a while, Cecile was inconsolable.

"I felt I had failed my husband because I wasn't able to give him a male heir. Emilio was very understanding. He said Helen was enough, that he loved her a lot. For a while, we thought of adopting a child, but scrapped the idea when the business expanded and took much of Emilio's time." A redeeming feature of this family is the parents' unconcealed love for each other, though one dominates the other.

Parents' Care for Child

Helen grew under the doting care of her parents and grandparents from both sides. She was a chubby, rosy-cheeked, cheerful girl everybody adored.

"She was treated like a princess and looked like one. She was so pretty we even entered her in a baby contest. She won the title 'Baby of the Month' and had free one-year supply of milk."

Busy as he was, Emilio never failed to give time to his wife and daughter. They went on out-of-town trips: to Batangas, to Cebu, to Davao. Once a year, the whole family went shopping in Hong Kong, and feasted on shark's fin and roasted duck. (Up to this day, Helen's favorite dish is Peking duck, Hong Kong style.)

Cecile, at this point, had her own concerns—she was selling insurance—but "it was such a light job, so I had enough time on my hands."

She spent much time cross-stitching, and trying new menus on her husband and daughter. "We had a cook at home, but when I was in the mood, I did the cooking myself. My specialty was Chinese food which my family loved and still does."

Spoiled and pampered, it is a wonder Helen did not become a brat.

"I wonder why," Cecile ponders. "We never really spanked her, but then we never felt a need for it. As for playmates, she was and still is, very close to her cousins."

Helen did well in school and got along with her teachers and peers.

"Her grades were excellent," Emilio proudly exclaims. "Even her conduct was flawless."

Little Helen would tag along with her father to the factory during weekends and vacations. The employees all liked her, and treated her like one of their own.

"Of course, we knew she was the boss' daughter," Paeng offers, "but it was never a barrier. The boss was very good to us, and Helen was—what would you call it—quite cute."

Paeng even recalled little Helen going over to him and wanting to sit in his lap, looking over his accounts. He would gladly oblige.

There was only one problem marring the picture: Helen was a sickly child. Though chubby, she was never as healthy as her parents wanted her to be. She had to be hospitalized a number of times as a child and had recurring bouts of asthma.

During these stressful times, Emilio and Cecile stayed with her in the hospital. They offered food to the gods for her recovery. (Both parents are Buddhists.) Fortunately, Helen always managed to recover. The parents' concern for Helen may go overboard, however, and she starts resenting it albeit much later. This family pattern of functioning will be reflected in the business, as we will soon see.

Enmeshment Problems in Family

The asthma became an issue when Helen wanted to take her master's degree abroad. At first, Emilio was adamant.

"What if something happened to her? She would be alone, and what if she got sick? The thought was terrifying to her mother and me."

Eventually, they compromised. Helen could go to Stanford, but she was to be accompanied by an aunt (Cecile's sister), whose lodgings were to be paid for in full by Emilio.

How did Helen feel about this?

"There were times, of course, when I felt Daddy was such a killjoy. Many of my friends are studying abroad, and they are not chaperoned. There were some things I wanted to do, you know, like partying and other such stuff, which I had to minimize because my aunt was there. It was no big deal, nevertheless. I was able to sneak out several times!"

After two years of study, Helen spent another year in the U.S. touring with her aunt. Then she returned to the Philippines, ready to work with her father. Evidently, too much enmeshment can cause problems in the family. How about in the business context?

Enmeshment Problems in Business

And that, she would say later, was when the trouble started. "I was being trained in the marketing department then, because that was my major in Stanford. I was having a nice time learning the ropes, and my immediate superior, Eugenio, was very experienced and understanding. I was learning a lot from him." The trouble is with her father.

"Eugenio left two years after I started working, and I was of course very honored that Daddy appointed me to his position. I know I am capable of doing well."

"The problem is—Daddy doesn't seem to think so. He has overruled decisions I have made more than five times already. He seems to think I am still his little girl who is going to climb on to his lap and ask for candy. I am a capable, grown woman, and he should realize that."

Did she ever tell this to her father?

"Oh, dozens of times. One time I even went to his room and came out disappointed. I knew my decision was the right one, but he overruled it."

What is Emilio's side of the story?

"I really think Helen still needs more experience. I know she performed well in school, but this is the business world. Things are different, and Helen is so idealistic. Sometimes, she would project something unrealistic."

How does he react to the charge that he does not acknowledge her adulthood?

He lets out a laughter, "Did she tell you that? Well, I don't know. If I didn't trust her enough, I wouldn't have appointed her in the first place. She still has to learn."

There is one other factor—Helen's health.

"Marketing is a tough job. Helen has to deal with clients, and even go out for client calls often. In this weather, with this pollution, she has been coughing more. I think she is working too hard, and she has to take a break sometimes."

Helen made a face when she heard this, but admitted that her father "has a point, but he shouldn't use it as an excuse."

Can she find an ally in her mother?

"Oh no," Helen moans, "Mommy totally agrees with Daddy. In fact, she didn't really want me to help in the business. She wants me to get married soon, and have a family of my own. Her dream is to have a dozen grandchildren." We see that similar enmeshment problems also occur in the business.

Succession Problems

How about the succession issue?

"As I said, I feel that Helen, with her health and inexperience, still cannot handle the business. Anyway, I am still strong. Don't get me wrong though. I have thought about the continuity of the firm. Hiroto and I have discussed it, and I think the key is to professionalize the company some more. Of course, Helen is always going to be a part of it—whether she continues with her position or not. She is going to be a major stockholder, and doesn't have to worry about the welfare of her own children when the time comes."

Helen counters, "I agree with Daddy's decision to professionalize more. We owe a lot to Eugenio and the rest. I just wish he would trust me more. I love him, but sometimes, he can be so frustrating."

Helen is still in the process of finding her own self, and stepping out from the shadow of her father. It is no wonder that succession is a problem.

Individuation patterns among the Chuas are shown below.

	Family	Business
Emilio	Close to wife and daughter; tends to overprotect daughter.	Appoints daughter to major position but often overrules her decisions.
Cecile	Close to husband and daughter; tends to overprotect daughter.	A board member but not involved in business operations; has own concern selling insurance.
Helen	Close to parents but feel they are too protective; trying to individuate.	Frustrated that father often overrules her decisions; trying to individuate.
Prevalent style	Enmeshed.	Enmeshed (where daughter is concerned); otherwise, egalitarian.

SFI Cohesion Subscale

Emilio and Cecile take pride in their family's closeness, but Helen feels that their togetherness is too much at times. The responses of the Chuas on the Cohesion Subscale are given below.

Item	Emilio	Cecile	Helen	Mean
2	1	1	2	1.3
15	1	1	2	1.3
19 (R)	1	1	2	1.3
27 (R)	1	1	2	1.3
36	3	3	2	2.7
Sum	7	7	10	8
Classification	Optimal	Optimal	Adequate	Adequate

SFI Expressiveness Subscale

Good communication links have been established in this family. A loving family, the members generally feel they can express themselves. Dissatisfied as Helen is sometimes, she acknowledges that she can be totally frank with her father. The scores of the Chuas on the Expressiveness Subscale are given below.

Item	Emilio	Cecile	Helen	Mean
1	1	1	3	1.3
9	2	2	2	2
13 (R)	2	2	2	2
20	1	1	2	2
22	1	1	2	2
Sum	7	7	11	9.3
Classification	Optimal	Optimal	Adequate	Optimal

SFI Style Subscale

The family is clearly centripetal in style, by its own admission. This is borne out by my observation and interviews with the members. Their scores on the Style Subscale are presented below.

	Emilio	Cecile	Helen	Mean
	2.56	2.56	2.59	2.57
Classification	MCP	MCP	MCP	MCP

Patriarchal Power in Family and Business

Emilio's power in the family is accepted by Cecile as well as Helen. However, Helen harbors some misgivings about her father's uncontested power in the business which impedes her individuation attemps.

Clear Dominance in Family and Business

Emilio is the power both in family and in business. His basis for power, though, is legitimate—and unquestioned by both wife and daughter. They admire his business acumen and his determination to provide a comfortable life for them, advantages which they are quick to point out and be grateful for. Even Helen, frustrated sometimes by what she feels is her father's "babyish" treatment of her, admits that she never dares go against him.

Did she ever attempt to do so?

"Once."

In college, Helen fell in love with a strong, handsome, intelligent gentleman named William. The only hitch was—he is a full-blooded Filipino, with nary an ounce of Chinese blood in him. Helen wept and railed, but her father was adamant.

"You very well know that your mother and I will never allow you to marry someone outside our race. Your grandmother would have a heart attack! I know William is a good man, but the cultural differences are too many. It can never work."

No amount of persuasion or rebellion could make him budge from his position. Did he ever threaten her, with say, disinheritance?

"No, Daddy would never do that. Actually, I think if I really wanted to, I could have disobeyed him and gone ahead with William. But at that time, it was too much trouble. And eventually, when I grew up, I outgrew William on my own. We were starting to have our own troubles."

Helen gave in and right now, can remarkably philosophize, "Looking back, I think Daddy was right. It could never have worked. William and I are still good friends, but that's about it."

The one situation wherein father and daughter reached a compromise was Helen's departure for Stanford for an MBA. Her aunt went with her, both a pro and a con from Helen's point of view.

"Of course, I thought Daddy was such a killjoy but I did see his point. I got sick around three times in those two years, and my aunt was the one who took care of me."

All in all, Helen considered the chaperoning to be worth it. Emilio was more quiet than her mother, Cecile, but he was the one in control.

"The few times Daddy got angry, even when it was not I he was angry with, I would get scared. I knew Mommy would be scared, too. We'd tiptoe around him, and she would try to humor him. Thank God it usually worked! They really are so sweet together and so demonstrative—unlike many Chinese couples, don't you think?" From the preceding accounts, we see that there is a clear power holder in the family as well as in the business—the patriarch.

Individuation and Power

It is in the business arena that Helen has butted heads with her father the most number of times.

"In this area, I don't want to give in because I think Daddy is being unreasonable. The excuses he gives are all just that—excuses. I think he just wants to pretend that I will be his little girl forever."

How does Helen react in this situation?

"I would go to his room and cry. Sometimes, I would shout at him. But it's difficult, you know. He just sits there with a smile even. I would get so frustrated I could scream!"

Did she ever try a more rational approach?

"Oh yes, I tried everything. I tried explaining to him, bargaining even; but he always says I need more time."

What about Emilio's assertion that Helen sometimes makes the wrong projections?

"Well, everybody makes mistakes. I bet Daddy had his own share of mistakes when he was just starting."

Does she have any tricks up her sleeve?

"I won't stop trying," Helen asserts. "He is my Daddy after all, and I know he has my welfare at heart. He will see my point of view, sooner than later, I hope."

Apparently, these complaints are not new to Emilio—he has confronted them all before. He nevertheless sticks to his rules.

"I have my reasons. I do not question Helen's competence in general, but she is still inexperienced. She has only been in the company for around five years, straight from school, without even working in another firm before joining us. And she is in a sensitive position—any major mistake will affect a lot of things."

So why did he appoint her there?

"Because it seemed right at that time, and I hoped it would make Helen happy. She was always so impatient. She wants everything at once." Individuation and power seemed to be related once more—an authoritarian power structure seems to be not conducive to successful individuation.

Succession Problems

Would succession be an issue?

"I want what is best for the continuity of the company. If Helen proves competent, of course, she will be the one to succeed. Right now, she is being trained somewhat. I won't hesitate to appoint another one, however, if he or she happens to be better qualified. I am clear in this—I don't want to be accused of nepotism. If Helen succeeds me, it is because she is qualified and not because she is my only child." Undoubtedly, that succession will be a problem.

How about his relationship with his wife?

"Cecile and I are very close and I will do anything for her. I love her dearly."

However, he admits that when push comes to shove, his wishes are to be obeyed. Doesn't Cecile ever question his authority? He does not think so.

She doesn't either.

"I am not that submissive, you know," Cecile laughs. "I follow him nevertheless because I think he is right. My husband is a highly intelligent and capable person. He always has sensible reasons for deciding this over that. Nonetheless he gives me the freedom to do my own thing, this insurance selling, for example."

So far, the relationships appear congenial enough. Will there be power struggles in the future? That possibility is not ruled out as long as father and daughter do not see eye to eye. Anyhow, the love and friendship they share seem strong enough to withstand any squabbles.

Exit Style

What is Emilio's possible exit style (Sonnenfeld 1988)? With his vision building and dedication, he is a monarch. With his caution regarding transitions, he is a general. With his openness to outside influences, he is an ambassador. His exit style is reflective of his leadership stance.

<u>Power relations</u> among the Chuas are summarized below.

	Family	Business
Prevalent style	Marked dominance.	Moderate dominance; style egalitarian with outsiders.
Power holder	Emilio.	Emilio.
Bases	Legitimate, referent, expert, informational, reward, coercive	Legitimate, referent, expert, informational, reward, coercive.
Processes	Strong assertiveness and control, authoritarian leadership but loving.	Strong assertiveness and control; professional leadership; flexible.
Outcomes	Acceptance and respect by wife and daughter, sometimes rebellion in daughter; cultural stereotyped roles.	Respect but daughter disappointed; limited by negotiations and problem-solving with daughter; good negotiation with outsiders.
Succession		Mixture of monarch, general, ambassador.

SFI Leadership Subscale

The Chuas know perfectly well who the boss is as the responses of Emilio, Cecile, and Helen on the Leadership Subscale show below.

Item	Emilio	Cecile	Helen	Mean
8 (R)	1	1	1	1
16	1	1	1	1
32	1	1	1	1
Sum	3	3	3	3
Classification	Optimal	Optimal	Optimal	Optimal

Close Nuclear Family Alliances

The marital as well as the nuclear family alliance is strong. The Chuas are very close to one another.

Strong Marital Alliance

Helen is an only child. The dynamics in this family are different: Evidently, the parents dote on Helen and are all the more protective of her. As we have seen, the marital alliance is strong, but the parental bond is cohesive and loving enough to include Helen.

Closeness to Child

Though tempting to posit, there seems to be no triangulation at work here. Because her father was so overprotective, Helen admits to trying to get her mother on her side, sometimes.

"It seldom worked. Mommy would agree with Daddy especially in matters concerning me. She would say it's for my own good."

How about conflict management? They are a loving family and care for each other. They do discuss matters and reach compromises, as evidenced by Helen's going abroad, with her aunt as chaperone. This state of affairs has still to be reached in the business sphere. As previously discussed, Emilio is the power here, and still has to show Helen he trusts her enough.

SFI Conflict Subscale

Even modifying the scale to account for item number 24, the members' responses indicate that, in general, they function fairly well together. Helen's discontent is clear and is tied up closely with her desire for differentiation. The responses of Emilio, Cecile, and Helen on the Conflict Subscale are given below.

Item	Emilio	Cecile	Helen	Mean
5 (R)	1	1	1	1
6	2	2	3	2.3
7	1	1	1	1
8 (R)	1	1	1	1
10 (R)	2	2	3	2.3
14 (R)	2	2	3	2.3
18 (R)	1	1	2	1.3
24 (R)	NA[a]	NA[a]	NA[a]	NA[a]
25 (R)	1	1	2	1.3
30 (R)	2	2	3	2.3
31 (R)	2	2	3	2.3
34	2	3	3	2.7
Sum	17	18	25	20
Classification	Adequate	Adequate	Midrange	Adequate

[a]Not applicable. #24 states: "One of the adults in this family has a favorite child." Helen is an only child.

Capable In-Law as Successor

The entry of in-laws will be difficult because of conditions set by Emilio. He will choose the in-law who, if qualified, will be a successor in the business.

Conditional Acceptance into Family

The Chua family is extremely centripetal. They care for each other deeply and prefer interacting and being with each other rather than dealing with other people. As we have seen, however, as Helen matures, she tries to individuate.

This may sound paradoxical because each family member has his or her own set of friends. Emilio is close to his Japanese partner and his senior management team. He plays golf with them. Cecile has her friends from high school and they sometimes go shopping, and exchange stories about raising children. Helen's friends are welcomed by her parents; she is also close to some of her cousins.

We can see here that outsiders are welcome as long as they fit into the Chua family's expectations and worldview.

Helen is taking her time and has not yet married; she has no steady boyfriend.

"I would rather remain single than rush into marriage unprepared. I am fortunate to live in an age where unmarried girls over the age of 25 are not ostracized!" she laughs.

Though her mother wishes for a dozen grandchildren, her father is not "pushing her in any way" to get married. On the contrary, he is critical of some of her suitors.

"Daddy is so *mapili* (choosy). He finds fault with one or the other. So it may be quite a while before I do get married!" (Recall that the father once vetoed a guy because he was not Chinese.) We can surmise that an in-law will be accepted by the Chuas—only conditionally—with the patriarch setting the terms.

Conditional Acceptance into Business

Will the in-law, if ever, be allowed to enter the business?

"If he could prove himself to be up to the challenge, why not? I have Paeng on the board so why not the husband of my daughter?" reasons Emilio.

Emilio has well-thought-out plans: If his son-in-law desires to enter and Emilio deems him to be capable enough, then he will be given a division to handle.

"We will see how it goes from there."

If not, then he will be trained first. A similar situation exists in the business: Acceptance is conditional.

Eligible Successor

Is the in-law a possible successor? Again, Emilio is very much open to this.

At present, he does not deem his daughter capable enough to manage the company, and is thinking along the lines of professionalizing the snack corporation altogether. Another option, of course, is to allow a trustworthy and proven son-in-law to take over. Similarly, the question of succession is conditional.

Professionals Treated as Family

Snackfoods Delights took in professionals early on during its growing years. They are even board members, and although not relatives, are treated as family.

Presence of Professionals

Emilio started the company with a foreign partner and things have worked out very well. Based in Japan, Hiroto would seldom take part in day-to-day affairs and trusted Emilio enough to handle things. He would fly to Manila from time to time especially during board meetings, and that was the extent of his participation.

From a partnership, the board has now expanded into six: Emilio and his family combined have the most number of shares (more than half) followed by Hiroto, with two professionals, Paeng and Tito, also having a part.

Expansion Purposes

As for professionals entering the business, Emilio said it was not a tough call to make. With his partner abroad and no child to help him then, he "really had no choice."

"I knew I had to get outside help."

So early on, he interviewed some people and chose Paeng, Tito, and Eugenio, all management graduates. Professionals, obviously, are accepted because the company wants to expand.

Respect for Founder

Relations between management and owner could not have been better.

"I don't even recall a time when we yelled at each other," marvels Emilio. "We agreed on most things."

Paeng shares this view.

"I keep on telling my wife that I am lucky to have such a nice boss. Emilio is easy to work with, and he is very dedicated. He drives himself hard and I think that is why all of us respect him that much. If he expects us to stay overtime, he himself will stay for even much longer. Certainly, he gives us good pay." The respect of the professionals for the founder clearly shows.

Trust Between Founder and Professionals

Over the years, the three managers have come to treat the corporation as "more like a family." They take great pride in its operations and are instrumental in some of the expansions. (Davis [1991] calls them "superstars," literally.)

"That was why I invited them into the board," Emilio explains. "They have already proven themselves. Without them, the company will not be where it is now." Trust is clearly manifested in the founder-professional relationship.

Professionals as Trainors

Helen was trained by Eugenio.

"I prefer a nonrelative to take charge of my daughter," Emilio says. "He can be less biased."

He admits he may not be objective enough in this area.

"Things have worked out just fine," Emilio continues. "Of course, I did not want Eugenio to leave, but he has his own family to think of. Helen has now taken his place."

Helen, however, is not given as much responsibility as Eugenio used to have. This aspect of the relationship between father and daughter has still to improve. In this family firm, the key role of professionals appears to be that of trainors.

Relationship with Other Employees

In the meantime, the company continues to grow. Senior management has its own junior managers to train and to take care of.

"Emilio is generally hands-off when it comes to our divisions. If a problem concerns one of my employees, the buck stops with me," Tito affirms.

Emilio meets with senior personnel who report to him directly. Under Paeng, Tito, and yes, Helen—there are also hierarchies of employees who report to them. The decision-making structure and trust between the founder and professionals are instrumental in the smooth relationship of the latter with the other employees.

Wide Exposure

One obvious reason the managers are so satisfied is that they have been given positions of responsibility. This coincides with Davis's (1990) research on the benefits received by professionals working for family firms. Because they have excellent relations with the owner, the situation remains ideal.

Eligible Successors

Are Paeng and Tito eligible for succession—even over Helen?

"If situation warrants it, why not?" Emilio reflects. "Right now, let's face it. They have more experience and expertise than my daughter. I think they will most likely manage the company better."

Helen is not to be left out, definitely.

"I have discussed this with her and I will make a place for her in the board. She does not have to worry because she will be amply provided for. Paeng and Tito do not have any objections."

In fact, Paeng thinks it is only fair.

"This is Emilio's company afterall. It is only right that his only child will have a big part of it. I would do the same in his place."

In Band's (1992) terms, the board is either going to be a caretaker board or a participative one with senior management making up a big part of it, and possibly will include other outsiders.

To the outsiders will go the management, and to Helen will go part of the ownership. How does she feel about this?

"Uncle Paeng and Uncle Tito are very close to our family and we owe them a lot. I think Daddy made a good decision to have them on the board. I don't mind."

She does hope, however, that her father would give her a more active role.

"Although I would want to be an owner, I also want to be part of the senior management team and run the company with the others." Whatever the future holds, it is worth noting that those trusted professionals are eligible successors.

Public Ownership

Does Snackfood Delights plan to go public?

"Oh yes, in fact, we are already making plans for a listing on the exchange, maybe, two or three years from now. It will give us the necessary capital to grow even more." With the good working relationships within the firm, public ownership is certainly welcome.

Affectionate Family and Business Functioning

Using Beavers Interactional Scales we can summarize the Chua family functioning thus:

1. *Structure of the family*
   a) Overt power: Marked dominance
   b) Parental coalition: Strong
   c) Closeness: Very close, often undifferentiated

2. *Mythology.* Generally congruent ("Family members should take care of each other.")

3. *Goal-directed negotiation.* Fair

4. *Autonomy*
   a) Clarity of expression: Generally clear
   b) Responsibility: Members regularly voice responsibility for individual actions, but sometimes blames others
   c) Permeability: Moderately open

5. *Family affect*
   a) Range of feelings: Direct expansion of many feelings despite some difficulty especially on part of child
   b) Mood and tone: Generally affectionate, warm, sometimes rebellious
   c) Unresolvable conflict: Some unresolved conflict with slight impairment of group functioning
   d) Empathy: Generally empathic, but not consistent

6. *Global health-pathology scale.* Low adequate (4)

The responses of the Chuas on the <u>Health/Competence Subscale</u> show that Emilio and Cecile (parents of Helen) feel the family is healthy as it is now; but Helen, although acknowledging their closeness, wants some changes. The table below has been adjusted to account for the inapplicability of item number 24.

Item	Emilio	Cecile	Helen	Mean
2	1	1	2	1.3
3	2	3	3	2
4	2	2	2	2
6	2	2	3	2.3
12	1	1	1	1
15	1	1	1	1.3
16	1	1	1	1
17	1	1	2	1.3
18 (R)	1	1	2	1.3
19 (R)	1	1	1	1.3
20	1	1	1	1
21	1	1	3	1.7
24 (R)	NA[a]	NA[a]	NA[a]	NA[a]
25 (R)	1	1	2	1.3
27 (R)	1	1	2	1.3
28	2	2	4	2.7
33	1	1	1	1
35	1	1	2	1.3
36	3	3	2	2
Sum	24	25	35	28
Classification	Optimal	Adequate	Adequate	Adequate

[a]Not applicable. #24 states: "One of the adults in this family has a favorite child." Helen is an only child.

Overall, Snackfood Delights' <u>business functioning</u> can be rated optimal, after assessing the detailed rating below following Dyer's (1986) checklist:

1. The founder is aware of the problems and tradeoffs the company is now facing and will face in the future.

2. The family has planned for future business needs.

3. There has been a relatively well-thought-out succession plan and this has been communicated to the relevant parties.

4. There are relatively well thought-out ownership options complementing the management succession plan.

5. The leader and his possible successors have an interdependent relationship, except for his daughter, whom he dominates.

6. An effective training program is in place for future managers and leaders.

7. Family and nonfamily members of the firm share similar views on equity and competence.

8. Problem-solving is still dominated by the founder, though decision-making is consensual with professional management.

9. The family handles conflict fairly well.

10. There are high levels of trust among family members as well as among family and nonfamily employees.

11. Outside feedback mechanisms are in place, primarily the presence of professional management and board members.

12. The family has a balanced perspective about family and business needs.

The Gotong Family: Garments House

Pacita Gotong, a widow (79 years old), was married to Benny Sr. (Gotong). They were blessed with three children: Benny Jr., now 58; Narcisa, now 55; and Simon, who died at age 44.

Benny Jr. is married with two sons—Paolo, 33, and Alex, 32. Narcisa, 55, is married to Greg Tangco, 57, and they have two children—Robert, 29, and Eileen, 27. Simon left a wife, Henrietta, 51, and two daughters—Michelle, 27, and Annabel, 24.

Pacita's brother, Henry Sr., used to be Benny Sr.'s trusted assistant in the business. Henry Sr.'s son, Henry Jr., is the same age as Simon and they used to be best friends. Henry Jr. is married to Marissa, an executive assistant in Garments House, the Gotong family enterprise.

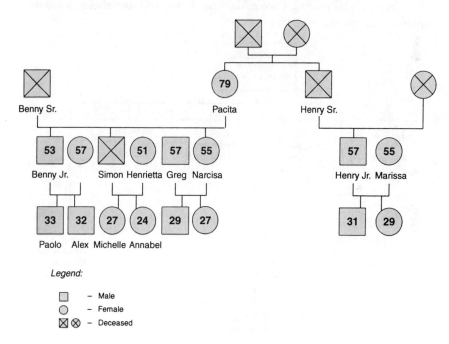

Legend:

◻ – Male
○ – Female
⊠ ⊗ – Deceased

The Gotong Family Genogram

Benny Jr., a physician, is president and chairman of the board of Garments House, a family firm founded by his father, Benny Sr. Pacita, his widowed mother, sits in the board as treasurer.

Paolo, Benny Jr.'s son, is executive vice-president and general manager; Greg Tangco, the husband of Narcisa, is a stockholder of Garments House; Narcisa, likewise, is stockholder. All three are members of the board.

Under Paolo, as the organizational chart shows, are Henrietta and Alex. Henrietta, the widow of Simon, is vice-president for administration. Alex, the other son of Benny Jr., is vice-president for marketing and concurrently board member.

Below Alex in the organizational ladder is Michelle, a daughter of Simon and Henrietta. Michelle is sales and marketing assistant. Equal in rank to her is Marissa, Henry Jr.'s wife, who serves as executive assistant to Benny Jr.

Narcisa, Henrietta, Paolo, Alex, Michelle, and Annabel graciously spared time for the interviews.

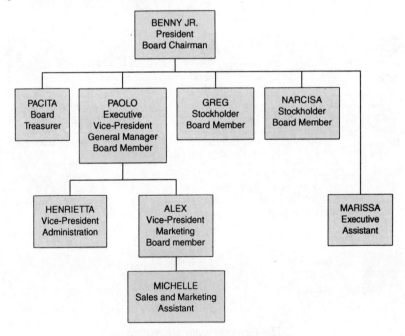

Garments House Organizational Chart

After World War II, Gotong decided to leave his native province of Canton in China for richer shores. His parents, a brother, and a sister were killed in a fire the previous year. His other surviving sister recently got married, and lived with her husband in the next town.

From his parents' stories, Gotong learned he had an uncle who lived in Binondo. He wrote his uncle, received an enthusiastic welcome and without further hesitation, 30-year-old Gotong crossed the Pacific to the Philippines.

To pay for his keep, Gotong helped his uncle in his small grocery store. Hardworking and pleasant, he attracted customers and soon earned their trust. One of them, Danny Ho, was about Gotong's age. The two became fast friends, and Danny soon broached to Gotong the idea of a garments business partnership.

With his uncle's blessings and an advance of ₱4,000, Gotong and Danny set up a partnership. Shares were to be split 50-50. With Danny's extensive contacts and Gotong's diligence, they converted a residence into a warehouse cum factory and invested in machines, compared textiles, and hired personnel. By maintaining excellent credit with suppliers, trustworthy relations with customers, hard work, and thrift, Garments House grew slowly but surely, steadily.

Gotong decided to adopt an Anglicized first name and chose Benny. A few months back, Benny was introduced to Pacita, a pretty Chinese whose parents immigrated from Fookien province some decades back. The match seemed perfect, they got married, and had three children in quick succession: Benny Jr., Simon, and Narcisa.

On Benny's preference, his wife took care of the household while he took care of the business, and it suited Pacita just fine. She raised the children practically on her own with the help of two nursemaids (yaya) while her husband ensured a secure lifestyle for the family.

In 1960, Danny decided to go into the flour industry and offered Benny Sr. his shares in the garments business. By this time, it was flourishing with three factories and around 120 employees making the partners far wealthier than they ever dreamed of. Benny Sr. readily bought Danny out, and the two parted amicably, no longer business associates but still great friends. With the business entirely in Gotong's hands, Benny Sr. decided to partition the shares equally among his family: himself, his wife, and his children.

Unlike many Chinese partriarchs, Benny Sr. did not encourage his children to help out in the business. Doing well in school was his priority for them, and nobody disappointed him. Benny Jr. became a physician, Simon an accountant, and Narcisa an architect. They were practicing their own professions and everything seemed perfect.

Besides, Benny Sr. had a trusted assistant—his brother-in-law, Henry Lim, Pacita's younger brother. Lured from a low-paying job in an electronics firm, Henry helped out in the garments business, drawing a steadily increasing salary. He was not given shares, but he did not really mind. His earnings in one month exceeded the salary he received in a year in his old job.

Henry had an only son, Henry Jr., the same age as Simon, Benny's son. The two children became best friends. While their parents worked in the factory, the cousins played and pretended to operate the machine pedals. Henry Jr. became an engineer.

Tragedy struck in 1965; a fire broke out in the biggest factory and the whole building was razed to the ground. Inventory was cut to one-fourth. Gritting his teeth, Benny Sr. decided to rebuild, this time with his second son Simon, the accountant, then 27, by his side. Simon became treasurer and chief finance officer.

Meanwhile, the youngest child, Narcisa, married her college sweetheart, Greg Tangco, the class topnotcher. Astute and driven, Greg impressed everyone he came in contact with, especially his father-in-law, Benny Sr.

Aggressive, dynamic, hard-driving, Greg might have reminded the old man of himself so many years ago, and Benny Sr. decided to recruit him with the promise of shares of stock. Greg agreed, and the company shares were redivided among six: four Gotongs, one Tangco, and one Gotong-Tangco.

Greg proved to be brilliant and was instrumental in the even more phenomenal growth of the company. Narcisa quit her architectural firm to be her husband's personal assistant. Meanwhile, the old man suffered a stroke and was in semiretirement. Simon and Greg seemed to get along well, and had their own separate responsibilities. Greg was soon promoted to general manager and executive vice-president.

Another in-law started working for Garments House. Simon's childhood friend Henry Jr. recently married Marissa, who passed the public accountancy exam with flying colors, landing in the top 30. Upon Henry Jr.'s recommendation and Benny Sr.'s blessings, Marissa became Simon's assistant. She was not offered shares, but she had no complaints about the salary and frequent perks. (The elder Henry died a year back and was deeply mourned by the clan especially Benny Sr.)

Ten years later, tragedy struck again. Benny Sr. suffered another stroke, and died at the age of 60. It was then that the succession issue reared its ugly head.

Already an up-and-coming physician, Benny Jr. conferred with his brother and his mother, and convinced them that he had to take his father's place. ("We are Gotongs, and we cannot let a Tangco take the reins.") During the next board meeting, Benny Jr. was voted president and chairman of the board. Greg remained vice-chairman, Simon treasurer, Narcisa secretary, and together with the elderly Pacita, retained their shares.

Greg did not take this decision lightly, and his beloved Narcisa sided with him. Quarrels erupted on all sides, earnings started dropping, employee morale suffered. Most of the rank and file agreed that Greg was the logical successor because Benny Jr. had never even set foot in the factories until his father's death. A physician by training, he did not have the minutest experience of running a major business.

As they say, tragedy strikes in threes and it did the third time in 1980. Simon, too, died of a heart attack at the tender age of 44, leaving his wife Henrietta and two daughters, Michelle and Annabel. The grieving matriarch, Pacita, took pity on her daughter-in-law and because of Henrietta's proven competence in her previous jobs (she had a degree in business management), decided to make her vice-president for administration. (Michelle would also become a sales and marketing assistant later on.)

Pacita also decided to take her son's place as treasurer. A homemaker most of her life, her previous experience was limited to voting and this time was no different.

"Her title is purely honorary," a grownup Annabel would say later. "Her job as treasurer was limited to signing checks placed in front of her."

Anyhow, Pacita was respected by her sons and daughter, so much so that in 1990, when Greg and Narcisa brought a lawyer to a board meeting and threatened to stake their claim, Pacita talked heart-to-heart with her only girl. Amidst much weeping, Narcisa bowed to her mother's will. After two months, she and Greg left to set up their own T-shirt business while remaining stockholders of Garments House.

The vacancy was promptly filled in by Benny Jr.'s eldest son Paolo, then 29. His other son Alex, then 28, became vice-president for marketing. (Their mother is a teacher and does not involve herself in the business.)

By this time, three generations were entrenched in Garments House: Pacita, Benny Jr. and his two sons, Henrietta and a daughter, Narcisa and Greg remaining stockholders; Marissa was promoted executive assistant (still without shares) to Benny Jr. Yet, the inexperience of the third generation, the squabblings among the second, and the helplessness of the first slowly proved to be detrimental to the business, to say the least.

Garments House is still one of the respected names in the business with ₱250 million in annual earnings (way below its heyday income), but the future looks hazy. No one can predict what will happen, and the third generation Gotongs are not happy with their positions.

Paolo and Alex have reportedly confided to their cousin Michelle, "We don't know what we are doing. We don't really like it here."

Inspite of their sentiments, they stay on because the business provides for them a house, a car, and the necessary luxuries of life.

"We really shouldn't complain much," Michelle, 27, opines. Her younger sister Annabel, 24, a first-hand witness to the strife among her elders, has been working in a bank since after graduation.

"I will never go into our family business. I have seen what harm it can do."

As for Narcisa and Greg, they maintain civil-enough relationships with the rest of the family (with the exception of Benny Jr.). Meanwhile, their own T-shirt business continues to grow. They have two children, Robert and Eileen, a dentist and a pediatrician. This branch of the younger generation does not harbor any ill will toward their cousins, but have decided to keep out of the fray.

(Pacita, Benny Jr., and Greg all declined to be interviewed. Among the second generation, I was able to talk only with Narcisa and Henrietta, but the third-generation Gotongs were more forthcoming. Paolo, Alex, Michelle, and Annabel were gracious and candid.)

Individuated But Too Independent

Individuated, the three Gotong children certainly are, but perhaps too independent of their parents and of each other.

Patriarchal Family Style

The marriage of Benny Sr. and Pacita was a rock-solid one, based on the comments made by the Gotongs.

"It was almost a match made in heaven," Narcisa remembers. "But it was typically Chinese. You know, my father makes most of the decisions, and my mother obeys him. She doesn't have any problems with that. I guess it's the culture they are used to."

Much has been written about the masculine predominance in Chinese society, and it is not our task to go into it here. Suffice it to say that this was a very likely situation.

Division of labor also worked well. Benny Sr. ruled the business while his wife raised the children almost single-handedly.

"We all respected our father," Narcisa reflects. "However, he was never really there for us. He is not a 'modern' father at all. Unlike the fathers you see today, he did not hug or kiss us. I don't remember going out to the movies or the park with him. I guess he was too involved in the business. I am not really complaining because I understand. All of us did. He was quiet and we were scared of him sometimes. It was our mother who took care of us."

What Benny Sr. cared about was his children's education.

"He made each of us show our report cards every quarter, and our grades had better be high!" Narcisa laughs. "If he was displeased, he did not scream but he kept very quiet, and he called all of us and lectured us on the virtues of diligence and perseverance. I remember getting angry at Simon often because his grades in social studies were not very high and we all got a lecture because of him!" The foregoing clearly illustrates a patriarchal family style.

With Pacita's daily mentoring, the children all graduated with honors, much to their father's satisfaction. They received small tokens then, such as a new dress, a new toy, or a new book.

Preferential Treatment in Family

The children were not exactly treated alike.

"I have always felt that our parents' favorite is Benny Jr. because he is the eldest, aside from being male. You know this preference Chinese have for males? He was also our grandparents' favorite, by the way, because he was the first grandson," Narcisa opines.

"I remember that during Christmas when we were given *angpao* (red Chinese-money envelope), I would always receive less money than my brothers. One time, I went to my mother and demanded to be told why, and she said, very matter-of-factly, it was because they are male and they would continue the family line. I am female and would get married someday and join another clan. I felt angry, but that was the way things were, and I couldn't do anything about it. Some of my friends in school had similar experiences."

So if Benny Jr. was the favorite, wasn't it only logical that he be the designated heir?

"I think our father wanted him to be, although he never said it explicitly. My brother, however, never had the inclination or the capacity, I think, to run a business. And my father saw that and never pushed him into it."

"My father is that kind of father, you know. Even if we were not that close, he never tried to run our lives. We were all allowed to do what we wanted as long as our grades were high. Anyway, it was my brother's childhood dream to be a doctor and he achieved it. Actually, we are all surprised that he insists on running the show now."

"I remember Simon telling me that when they were young, he and his brother played 'doctor-doctor' and Benny was always the doctor. He was always in command, and Simon was always a bit in awe of him. Benny was more aggressive, always got his own way, and was the favorite of his parents and grandparents. As the eldest, he always got the newest books, the newest clothes, the newest everything. Simon got the hand-me-downs," Henrietta muses. It is clear that culturally-generated preference operates in the family as it would in the business later on.

Patriarchal Business Style

Their mother Pacita had always been in the sidelines supporting her husband, and when he died, the next patriarch in line was her eldest son, Benny Jr. We can see here that business is an extension of the family—a patriarchal mode in one follows from the other.

Preferential Treatment in Business

"For my mother, it is my eldest brother who is taking our father's place. She listens to him and obeys his every wish."

"Our relationship with each other was fair enough, I suppose," Narcisa reflects. "We were never really close. We had our own friends and Simon was particularly close to our cousin Henry Jr." Evidently the preferential treatment in the family spills over to the business.

Individuation in Next Generation

Even Benny Jr.'s sons volunteer similar observations about their father. Company culture is certainly, in Dyer's (1986) terms, paternalistic with one dominant head.

"Our father can be dominating at times," says Paolo. "I would hear him ordering the employees about and even shouting at them. As for us, we were never really close either. He was so busy in his clinic that he left us alone. We never really had much contact with him until now that he wants us to work with him in Garments House."

"We really shouldn't be complaining," laughs Alex. "Because of him, we never lack for anything in life. All the luxuries we are enjoying now come from his share in the family business and his earnings as a doctor."

How do they feel about being in the business? Paolo and Alex stole glances at each other.

"Not too happy," Paolo reveals. "In fact, Alex and I are not really business inclined. We graduated from engineering, and we would really like to practice it. Yet our father wants us to stay here, and I guess this is where we should stay."

It is admittedly the earnings from the business that could bring them comfort and good life that keeps them in Garments House. Aside from that, they defer to their father's wishes because they are scared of him.

"This is really a bad thing to say," Alex confides to me, "but I think you can understand because you are also Chinese. Our father has threatened to cut us off if we do not obey him. We would rather not cause trouble."

As for the rift between their father and their Aunt Narcisa, both boys say it is sad, but they are helpless.

(Both insist that as brothers, they are close enough. "We go out on double dates, and we go bar hopping," Paolo says. "Alex is okay.")

They are a lot closer to Simon's daughters, Michelle and Annabel, than to Narcisa's and Greg's children, Robert and Eileen. Michelle works with them in the business, and shares a similar sentiment.

"I don't feel like working there much longer especially because my mother can never be a stockholder. I am in good terms with Paolo and Alex, but I don't like Uncle Benny. He is difficult to get along with, and is very temperamental."

Even Henrietta says that her days in Garments House are numbered. She would like to go out and start another business with her daughters. Apparently, they are a very close-knit family especially after her husband Simon died.

"Ma is wonderful," enthuses Annabel, "we can always go to her and tell her anything. I know Paolo and Alex are envious because they cannot do the same with their father or their mother."

The two girls were brought up in a caring and loving home. Simon was a dutiful father, and "he never neglected us. He used to tell us that he would never be a distant father because he experienced it himself and didn't like it," Michelle says. It was a big shock for the family when he died.

"For more than a year, Ma was inconsolable. She really loved him and he, her," Annabel becomes teary-eyed. "Michelle and I had to take care of her for a while."

The two girls insist that they are the best of friends—and their mother is definitely included. As for their other cousins, Robert and Eileen, "well, because of the grownups' quarrel, we rarely get to see them that much. We would like too, though. During clan reunions, they come and everything is normal but only on the surface. I knew there was always something underneath. If you ask us, we think no one can go against Uncle Benny."

Regarding her own family, Narcisa says she maintains a close relationship with her children. Sharing Simon's sentiment, she replies that she wants parents who are "warmer and more sensitive" and vows to be that way with her own.

Individuation patterns for Benny Sr.'s family are summarized below.

	Family	Business
Benny Sr.	Close to wife but always dominant, could not let her fully differentiate from him; distant with children generally, but closer to eldest son; lets children go their own way.	Did not let wife participate during his lifetime; secretly wished eldest son would take over but did not train him for succession; worked well enough with second son and in-laws.
Pacita	Close and submissive toward husband, could not fully differentiate; closest to eldest son, submissive toward him after husband's death.	Joined only after husband and second son died; now holds a title but no real power; obeys eldest son's wishes.

Continued next page

Continued from preceding page

	Family	**Business**
Benny Jr.	Favorite of parents, often got his way; used to being in command and the center of attention; independent enough from father in terms of relationships and career, but mother finds it difficult to differentiate from him; distant from own family.	A practising physician but wants control of business with mother's support; alienated sister and brother-in-law; no previous experience in running the business.
Simon	Independent enough but in awe of elder brother; had own family and practiced child-rearing methods different from the way he was reared; close to wife and children.	Joined family firm but father made most of the decisions; toed the line.
Narcisa	Independent from parents and siblings; distant from brother and mother but respects mother; close to her own family.	Took husband's side against brother and mother; now runs own business with husband.
Prevalent style	Generally disengaged.	Dominated by Benny Sr. then, Benny Jr. now.

For Benny Jr.'s family's individuation patterns:

	Family	Business
Benny Jr.	Distant from wife and sons; sometimes uses threats to make children obey him; respected but feared by sons.	Made sons take over vacancies on board but does not let them make major decisions.
Benny Jr.'s wife	Pursues her own interests; distant from husband and sons.	Not involved in business.
Paolo	Distant from parents; fears father's control over inheritance; has to follow father; not individuated; close to brother.	Has to follow father; cannot make major decisions; not individuated.
Alex	Distant from parents; fears father's control over inheritance; has to follow father; not individuated; close to brother.	Has to follow father; cannot make major decisions; not individuated.
Prevalent style	Disengaged.	Disengaged.

And for Simon's family's individuation patterns:

	Family	Business
Simon	Close to wife and daughters; loved and respected by them.	Did not force daughter to join business but elder one decided to.
Henrietta	Close to husband and daughters; loved and respected by them.	Joined after husband died but cannot have shares; plans to leave.
Michelle	Close to parents and sister; individuated.	Joined business but cannot make decisions; plans to leave.
Annabel	Close to parents and sister; individuated.	Works outside and has no intention of joining company.
Prevalent style	Individuated.	Individuated.

Narcisa's SFI Cohesion Subscale

Narcisa, the only daughter, sees her family as more disengaged than enmeshed, with members going their separate ways most of the time. Narcisa's scores for her family of origin for the Cohesion Subscale are given below.

Item	Narcisa
2	4
15	4
19 (R)	4
27 (R)	4
36	3
Sum	19
Classification	Borderline

Narcisa's SFI Expressiveness Subscale

Narcisa perceives the favoritism in the family but feels helpless in doing anything about it. The siblings are independent but maybe too much so. They often tend to act without regard for each other. Narcisa's scores on the SFI Expressiveness Subscale are given below.

Item	Narcisa
1	4
9	5
14 (R)	3
20	4
22	4
Sum	20
Classification	Borderline

Narcisa's SFI Style Subscale

Narcisa's score (2.35) for SFI Style is classified as moderate centripetal.

Beavers's computational formula for SFI style may not be applicable here. Item number 4 ("The grownups in this family understand and agree on family decisions"), which accounts for a sizable factor in this computation, may have been the cause: The grownups do agree on family decisions because the mother always gives in to the father. Based on observations and comments of the interviewees, this family tends to be more centrifugal than centripetal.

Paolo's and Alex's SFI Cohesion Subscale

The brothers Paolo and Alex reveal that they are not close to their parents but nevertheless maintain good ties with them. This is confirmed by their responses on the SFI Cohesion Subscale as presented below.

Item	Paolo	Alex	Mean
2	3	3	3
15	4	3	3.5
19 (R)	3	3	3
27 (R)	3	3	3
36	3	3	3
Sum	16	15	15.5
Classification	Midrange	Midrange	Midrange

Paolo's and Alex's SFI Expressiveness Subscale

Alex and Paolo apparently wish they can express themselves freely without fear or threat of disinheritance. This is reflected in their responses on the Expressiveness Subscale as presented below.

Item	Paolo	Alex	Mean
1	3	3	3
9	5	4	4.5
13 (R)	3	3	3
20	4	3	3.5
22	4	4	4
Sum	19	17	18
Classification	Borderline	Midrange	Borderline

Paolo's and Alex's SFI Style Subscale

As for style, Paolo's score (on a scale of 1 to 5) for the SFI Style is 2.92; Alex's is also 2.92. Both scores are classified as MCP (moderate centripetal).

A score of 3 is considered "mixed" in the American context and we see how close to this the brothers' scores are. Their father makes most of the decisions but generally, parents and sons go their own separate ways.

Simon's Family's SFI Cohesion Subscale

Regarding their own nuclear family, the responses of Henrietta, Michelle, and Annabel on the Cohesion Subscale are presented in the table below.

Item	Henrietta	Michelle	Annabel	Mean
2	2	2	2	2
15	2	2	2	2
19 (R)	2	2	2	2
27 (R)	2	2	2	2
36	3	3	3	3
Sum	11	11	11	11
Classification	Adequate	Adequate	Adequate	Adequate

This family is very close-knit, they even respond alike. Their cohesiveness is demonstrated not only by their responses but also by their actions. During the interview, they touched one another and seemed openly affectionate.

Simon's Family's SFI Expressiveness Subscale

All the members trust each other enough to be able to express themselves freely, all the while treating each other with respect and tenderness. The scoring for their responses on the SFI Expressiveness Subscale below reflect this.

Item	Henrietta	Michelle	Annabel	Mean
1	1	1	1	1
9	1	1	1	1
13 (R)	1	1	2	1.3
20	1	1	1	1
22	1	1	1	1
Sum	5	5	6	5.3
Classification	Optimal	Optimal	Optimal	Optimal

Simon's Family's SFI Style Subscale

The members scored 2.34 classified as MCP (moderate centripetal) in the SFI Style Subscale. All three admit to being the best of friends and their scores validate this.

Illegitimate Power

All was well with the Gotongs when the acknowledged power was also respected. Trouble began when the new power took over. He does not have the respect of siblings who perceive that he lacks the necessary expertise in the family business.

Ambivalent Power Structure

Benny Sr. and Pacita decided early on to apportion their respective spheres of influence: He would have authority over the business and she over the family. Did this division work?

It worked for a while in the business. Benny Sr. was free to concentrate on expanding his empire, caring little for the upbringing of his children, save for the occasional lecture on the significance of education, and, of course, the constant pressure on him to provide a more comfortable life for them all. It is easy to discern that the power structure can only be considered legitimate as long as the acknowledged authority is respected. The absence of respect would result in power struggles.

Moderate Dominance

Benny Sr.'s partner deferred to him because he was the founder of the business, aside from being charismatic. He was given a virtually free hand by his trusting business partner to run it well. Consequently, Benny Sr. exercised almost absolute control over every aspect of Garments House. This power was acknowledged and accepted by everyone, particularly outsiders. Henry Sr. was Benny Sr.'s good friend who, like everybody else, acknowledged the latter's authority.

"He had the skills, he had the expertise; he was the most dedicated of them all," Narcisa asserts. "Certainly, everyone recognized his authority. They should."

The snags in the senior Gotong's leadership were the tragic fires and deaths. Otherwise, business was fine, as can be gleaned from the interviews.

When Greg entered the firm, part of Benny Jr.'s authority was vested on him with the old man's blessing. He soon earned the respect of the employees because they recognized his expertise and knowledge plus his dedication and fairness. When he left, there was a general sentiment that it was an unfortunate move for Garments House.

The power, with attendant negative consequences, resides with Benny Jr. Essentially, many view his acquisition of authority as illegitimate. As a result, morale suffered as it still does. Even his own sons admit it.

"I think our father is better off being a doctor than a businessman," reflects Paolo.

Alex just smiles opting not to say it too loud or too often. Inspite of their fancy titles, Benny Jr.'s two sons feel relatively powerless.

"It is our father who makes the decisions even though we are members of the board and management."

At times, they find it frustrating; but then again, they cannot complain too loud.

"The money from Garments House affords us our present comfort and state of life. I guess we should not bite the hand that feeds us, wouldn't you say?"

"I don't know. I think he always has this urge to be on top," says Alex, analyzing his father.

Narcisa agrees in her own way. The ambivalent feelings come as no surprise, given the ambivalent power structures prevalent in the family and business.

Cultural Norms in Family

"Benny Jr. has always been our parents' and grandparents' favorite, being the eldest male and all. He always got the best things and got used to them. He acts as if the world revolves around him and expected everybody to bow to his wishes." These cultural norms are observed in the family as well as in the business. This is the realm of the family. Couldn't Pacita have done something about this seeming inequity?

Cultural Norms in Business

"You have to understand. My mother is of the old school. She prefers boys to girls. It is something I have learned to accept and I am not bitter. I love her and respect her nonetheless because she has been a good mother. When our father died, it is as if his influence over the family was handed over to his namesake."

Although Narcisa accepted her parents' authority, she cannot accept her brother's. She thinks he has not proven himself at all.

What about Simon, the middle one?

"Simon has always been the one who did not want to cause trouble. He was in good terms with both Benny and me; Benny, because he deferred to him, and I, because he was kind to me in general. He had his own friend, Henry Jr., and the two were always together."

Power Structure in Next Generation

Simon's widow Henrietta smiles assuringly. She vows not to let this state of affairs run into the next generation of her own family.

"In our family, decision-making is shared. When Michelle and Annabel were still kids, Greg and I made the major decisions for them, naturally. We would do it after a thorough discussion. After reaching a compromise pleasing to both of us, we approached the children together. I read somewhere that it is best for parents not to quarrel in front of the children so we made sure that we settled things first before talking to them."

Annabel agrees, "I think Michelle and I are very lucky to be this close to our parents. When we did something wrong as children, our parents would punish us, of course—usually with two or three slaps. Afterwards, they explained things to us until we understood. Michelle and I never rebelled; we never had to. Ma and Pa gave us enough room, and they were there when we needed them."

What about Narcisa's own family?

"We are close. I don't want Robert and Eileen to be at each other's throats like Benny and I are now. Greg and I share in the major decisions, and because the children have matured, they make their own. Shouldn't it be that way?"

Paolo and Alex listen attentively.

"Our mother is not strict at all so we were never afraid of her. We love her, but well, we don't really obey her when we don't feel like it. And it seems *okey lang* (just all right) with her. We are scared of our father, but in the family, we stay out of his way. I guess all of us just observe the motto: live and let live."

What about decision-making?

"Paolo and I make our own decisions. If we have a problem, we consult with each other; very rarely do we consult with our mother, and with our father, never. That's just the way things are."

Exit Style

Let us now analyze the different exit styles (Sonnenfeld 1988) in Garments House. For the first generation, Benny Sr. acted more like a mixture of monarch and general. For the second, Greg was like a general, and would have been an ambassador save for his unceremonious ouster. Benny Jr., currently the power holder, does not fit any classification because the legitimacy of his claim remains questionable. Their exit styles are reflective of their leadership modes and ways of relating with other.

Power relations in the Gotong family and business are summarized below.

	Family	Business
Prevalent style	Moderate dominance then, but chaotic now.	Marked dominance then and now, but also chaotic now.
Power holder	Pacita then, now ambivalent.	Benny Sr. then, Benny Jr. now.
Bases	Legitimate, reward, coercive.	Benny Sr.: legitimate, referent, expert, reward, informational; Benny Jr.: coercive.
Processes	Moderate assertiveness and control; unstable and weak leadership.	Benny Sr.: strong assertiveness and control; egalitarian with outsiders; flexible. Benny Jr.: strong assertiveness; little control; authoritarian.
Outcomes	General affection of family; stereotyped roles; resentment by daughter; estrangement among siblings; poor negotiation and problem-solving strategies.	Benny Sr.: good negotiation and problem-solving strategies; rules generally enforced. Benny Jr.: unpredictable consequences; poor negotiation and problem-solving strategies; employee morale is low; business suffering; estrangement among siblings.
Succession		Benny Sr.: mixture of monarch and general; Benny Jr.: still in doubt.

It may also be instructive to look at the power relations in **Benny Jr.**'s and Simon's nuclear families. The next table summarizes <u>power relations</u> in Benny Jr.'s family.

	Family	Business
Prevalent style	Laissez-faire, often chaotic.	Marked dominance.
Power holder	Benny Jr.	Benny Jr.
Bases	Legitimate, reward, coercive.	Coercive.
Processes	Strong assertiveness; little control; inflexible.	Strong assertiveness and control; inflexible.
Outcomes	Distancing of wife and sons; fair problem-solving; poor negotiation with children; rules by father obeyed out of fear; rules by mother ignored.	Compliance by children; poor problem-solving strategies and negotiation; frustration of children.
Succession		Still in doubt.

Power relations in Simon's family are summarized next.

	Family	Business
Prevalent style	Egalitarian.	Egalitarian.
Power holder	Simon, then Henrietta (after Simon's death).	Benny Sr. then, Benny Jr. now.
Bases	Legitimate, referent, expert, informational, reward, coercive.	Benny Sr.: legitimate, referent, expert, reward, informational. Benny Jr.: coercive.
Processes	Moderate assertiveness and control; democratic leadership; flexible.	Benny Sr.: strong assertiveness and control; egalitarian with outsiders; flexible. Benny Jr.: strong assertiveness; little control; authoritarian.
Outcomes	Good negotiation and problem-solving strategies; love and respect of wife and daughters; role sharing; rules usually enforced.	Benny Sr.: good negotiation and problem-solving strategies; rules generally enforced. Benny Jr.: unpredictable consequences; poor negotiation and problem-solving strategies; employee morale is low; business suffering; estrangement among siblings.

Narcisa's SFI Leadership Subscale

Narcisa feels that clear leadership is lacking in her family of origin as reflected in her responses on the Leadership Subscale—4 for all three items, classified as borderline.

Paolo's and Alex's SFI Leadership Subscale

What about Benny Jr.'s family? The responses of Paolo and Alex (second-generation Gotongs), Benny Jr.'s sons, parallel the responses of Narcisa (first-generation Gotong) on the SFI Leadership Subscale. The responses of Paolo and Alex are classified as borderline as shown in the table below.

Item	Paolo	Alex	Mean
8 (R)	4	5	4.5
16	4	3	3.5
32	4	4	4
Sum	12	12	12
Classification	Borderline	Borderline	Borderline

Simon's Family's SFI Leadership Subscale

The table confirms Henrietta's vow of making her own family's relationships less chaotic. The responses of Henrietta, Michelle, and Annabel on the Leadership Subscale are shown below.

Item	Henrietta	Michelle	Annabel	Mean
8 (R)	1	1	1	1
16	2	2	2	2
32	3	3	2	2.6
Sum	6	6	5	5.7
Classification	Adequate	Adequate	Adequate	Adequate

Poor Sibling Relationships

The Gotong siblings resented the unconcealed favoritism heaped on Benny Jr. As a result, the poor sibling relationships among them is wreaking havoc on the business.

Strong Marital Alliance but Wife Lacks Identify

Benny Sr. is the acknowledged leader in his strong marital bond to Pacita. Brought up in a culture where wives have to be subservient to their husbands (and later on to their eldest sons), Pacita was not resentful. She gave her love and devotion to her husband until his dying day. He, for his part, reciprocated by doing his duty toward her and to his family by providing a comfortable life for them. (We cannot surmise what would have happened had Pacita been more assertive.) The marital alliance is strong but, apparently, it is made so at the expense of the individuality of one parent.

Preferential Treatment by Parents

By mutual consent, Benny Sr.'s domain was the office, Pacita's, the home. Pacita, however, did not oversee her domain with a big stick. She took care of her children as best as she could, but she never hid her preference for the eldest male child, Benny Jr., the "precious namesake" of her husband. Benny Jr. received preferential treatment over all the other siblings.

Differentiation as Sibling Function

In the section on individuation, we have seen how Narcisa resented the favoritism heaped on Benny Jr. She went to her mother and demanded to know why her elder brother received more gifts than she did, only to be rebuffed with "this is the way it should be."

"Oh, there were many instances, too many to recount," Narcisa says. "It was very clear; from my grandparents, both maternal and paternal, to my own parents, everyone fawned over Benny Jr. He was the pet and got the best of everything."

How about Simon, the second?

"Oh, he got more than I did, because he is also male, but always less than Benny's, because Simon is only the second. The eldest always gets the most inheritance at the end."

As a result, Narcisa became assertive.

"I tried to do well in school so that my parents would be very proud of me," she remembered. "I succeeded, but Benny also did well. I don't think I could ever win anything over him."

Simon bowed out of the competition.

"Simon was always the nicest among all of us," Narcisa muses. "Maybe that was why he died so young. Do you know the Chinese saying: the good die young? Well, Simon was one of those. He was so easygoing that he got along with me and my brother. Benny and I were never close, but Simon would play with both of us—separately, of course. I guess that was because he would always give in." Differentiation is the dominant sibling function in the family and is also mirrored in the business.

Poor Sibling Relationships in Family

We can see that Benny Jr., among the siblings, was supposedly the holder of power bestowed on him by parents, by virtue of his gender and cultural norms. Narcisa perceived this influence as illegitimate and tried to undermine it by coercion. Simon tried to keep peace, and always acted as mediator, and turned to an outsider, his cousin Henry Jr., who became his best friend.

Poor Sibling Relationships in Business

This childhood sibling rivalry extends to the business. At first, Narcisa thought everything was fine because Benny Jr. started practicing medicine, and did not seem to want to join Garments House. With Simon and her husband Greg there, the future looked rosy for Narcisa. Imagine her shock when Benny Jr. ousted Greg from what "everybody felt to be Greg's rightful place," and installed himself and his two sons instead. The shock was compounded by Narcisa's discovery of her mother's siding with the "usurper."

"I wasn't really surprised. It was in character for my mother to side with the eldest male. She has always been indecisive."

Yet Narcisa had enough respect for her mother not to cause anymore trouble. After an emotional discussion, she and Greg left the business while retaining their shares, but relinquishing all management privileges.

"After all, she is still my mother."

The estranged siblings have become barely civil to each other especially in front of their mother during family reunions which are usually "strained affairs," as Narcisa notes. Her nieces Annabel and Michelle agree. The concurring sentiments show that the poor sibling relationships in the family affect the business.

Succession Problems

No one can predict the future. Even Benny Jr.'s sons are hesitant to take over. Not individuated enough from their father, fearful of him yet wanting to hold on to the luxury the business brings, Alex and Paolo seem to be at a loss. Michelle and Annabel, having grown up in a more congenial atmosphere, have made up their minds: Michelle will not stay long, and Annabel will never enter the "battlefield." With chaotic family alliances, succession is definitely a problem.

Sibling Relationships in Next Generation

How are sibling relationships among the younger generation?

"Paolo and I are close," Alex says. They have to be, as a reaction against their dominating father and weak mother. "Sometimes, we side with our mother, but most often, we don't want to cause trouble. Our parents are not very close, but they seem all right most of the time. I think it is best that we keep it that way."

As for Michelle, "My mother, Annabel, and I are the best of friends." With their father Simon gone so early, the three have decided to support and care for each other.

Sibling relationships and other nuclear family alliances in the Senior Gotong's family are shown below.

	Family	Business
Marital alliance	Strong, cohesive, consistent; husband clearly dominant.	Wife not involved when husband was alive, but always supportive of him.
Parent-child	Favoritism toward eldest son; fair relationships with others.	Simon and Narcisa treated fairly by father, but after father's and Simon's death, mother sided with eldest son.
Sibling relations	Rivalry between eldest son and daughter, middle child as mediator; functions: different-iation, dealing with parents by tattling.	Good relationship between Narcisa and Simon but conflict between her and Benny Jr.; rivalry and bitterness between Narcisa and Benny Jr.

How about Benny Jr.'s nuclear family? Their relationships are shown below.

	Family	Business
Marital alliance	Fair.	Wife not involved in business.
Parent-child	Distant, children left on their own; perceived as unloving by children.	Children not allowed to make major decisions; children frustrated but fearful of causing trouble.
Sibling relations	Very close; functions: deals with parents by balancing and colluding, mutual regulation, direct services, good negotia-tion and problem-solving.	Very close; functions: deals with father by balancing, mutual regulations.

The table below summarizes the relationships in Simon's family.

	Family	Business
Marital alliance	Strong, cohesive, consistent.	Wife only joined after husband's death, but supportive of him then.
Parent-child	Close and loving, perceived as fair.	Close; mother and daughter help one another in business.
Sibling relationships	Close; functions: regulation, direct business services, good negotiation and problem-solving.	One sister not involved in business.

Narcisa's SFI Conflict Subscale

Narcisa is dissatisfied with the way her family handles conflict, as shown by her responses on the SFI Conflict Subscale below.

Item	Narcisa
5 (R)	1
6	3
7	3
8 (R)	4
10 (R)	5
14 (R)	4
18 (R)	3
24 (R)	5
25 (R)	3
30 (R)	4
31 (R)	4
34 (R)	3
Sum	42
Classification	Borderline

Paolo's and Alex's SFI Conflict Subscale

Paolo and Alex try not to antagonize the power holder, their father, but feel that conflict management in their family is only fair at most. This is confirmed by their responses on the SFI Conflict Subscale below.

Item	Paolo	Alex	Mean
5 (R)	3	3	3
6	4	4	4
7	3	3	3
8 (R)	4	5	4.5
10 (R)	3	3	3
14 (R)	3	3	3
18 (R)	3	3	3
24 (R)	1	1	1
25 (R)	3	3	3
30 (R)	4	4	4
31 (R)	3	3	3
34	2	3	2.5
Sum	36	38	37
Classification	Midrange	Midrange	Midrange

Simon's Family's SFI Conflict Subscale

The responses of Henrietta, Michelle, and Annabel (Simon's family), on the SFI Conflict Subscale paint a totally different picture compared to those of Narcisa's and the sons of Benny Jr.

Item	Henrietta	Michelle	Annabel	Mean
5 (R)	1	1	1	1
6	1	1	1	1
7	1	1	1	1
8 (R)	1	1	1	1
10 (R)	1	1	1	1
14 (R)	1	1	1	1
18 (R)	1	1	1	1
24 (R)	1	1	1	1
25 (R)	1	1	1	1
30 (R)	1	1	1	1
31 (R)	2	3	2	2.3
34	1	2	1	1.3
Sum	13	15	13	13.6
Classification	Optimal	Optimal	Optimal	Optimal

Competent In-Law as Outsider

As long as the in-law does not prove to be a threat to the power, his or her relationship with the power holder is congenial. Otherwise, a struggle for power ensues, with family members elbowing out an in-law who is qualified as a successor.

Acceptance into Family and Business

During Benny Sr.'s time, extended family members were welcomed into the business if they demonstrated a capability and willingness to join. Henry Sr. is one prime example—he and the senior Gotong got along very well, and he was also instrumental in the company's growth during the early years. He did not have shares but occupied a senior management position anyhow. This was the state of affairs when Henry Jr.'s wife Marissa entered the company initially as Simon's assistant. This proved to be a good move because Henry Jr. and Simon were best friends.

What is most interesting, of course, is the entry of Greg Tangco. When Narcisa married Greg, it was with the approval and acceptance of her parents. Greg comes from a decent Chinese family, is respectful of his elders, and is very intelligent besides. Benny Sr. took a liking to him and offered him a place in the business which Greg accepted. Observe that as long as the legitimate power holder (the founder) accepts the in-law, there is no problem.

Founder and Capable In-Law

For the first few years, it seemed a wise choice. Greg got along with Simon and the rest. The employees looked up to him because he was humble and had no airs. Extremely dedicated and hardworking, he earned the employees' respect and, according to Henrietta, also their affection. Even Benny Jr. caused no trouble, at first.

"He and Greg were not particularly close, but then of course, my brother and I never really got along. At least, on the surface, they were civil to each other. On my wedding day, my brother was there, and I remember he even congratulated Greg and welcomed him to our family," Narcisa reminisces. Even when Greg rose to be the senior Gotong's right-hand man, Benny Jr. did not seem to mind.

We can see that because the in-law has proven himself, he is welcomed into the business.

Problems with In-Law Entry into Business

The power struggle in Garments House was bitter with one side even threatening to bring the affair to court. This was stopped only out of respect for the surviving matriarch, Pacita. Narcisa seems resigned now.

"Maybe it's for the best. At least Greg and I got out from where there was animosity on all sides. Our business is doing fine and our family is harmonious."

What caused Benny Jr. to oust his brother-in-law? I could not get his side for he refused to be interviewed. He reportedly wanted to preserve the company under the Gotong family name. Evidently, Greg is perceived as an outsider despite his competence and because he is married to a sister Benny Jr. does not particularly get along with, Benny Jr. has all the more reason to seize power.

The other in-laws and relatives are still in place, perhaps because they possess relatively little power and certainly pose no threat. Henrietta, Simon's widow, remains vice-president for administration. After Simon's death, Marissa was handpicked by Benny Jr. himself to be his executive assistant.

How do Henrietta and Benny Jr. get along? She hesitates, "I have seen firsthand the friction between Greg and Benny. I don't want to get involved. Actually, I am happy in my position and I don't need to go any higher. When Simon was alive, he was content with what he had, too."

"I get along with Benny just fine, but I am careful not to go over his head or hide anything from him. Sometimes, I try to guide him because he really needs help. After all, he studied medicine, not business. When I do help him, he doesn't seem to mind. He is even grateful."

"He treats me and the children well enough. Every Christmas, we receive something from him—ham for the family and some angpao for the children. So far, we are on friendly terms."

Michelle is quick to agree, but she has no plans of staying long. She and Annabel plan to start a business on their own, most likely with their mother.

As for Paolo and Alex, they have confided to their cousins that they "don't really like it here" but may have to stay put for the time being. On the whole, as long as sibling relationships are chaotic to begin with, the entry of an in-law would complicate matters.

Professionals and Other Outsiders

Managerial positions will be filled up by family members, not professionals, definitely. Nonrelatives do not make major decisions in Garments House.

Absence of Professionals

There are no professionals in managerial positions, even in Benny Sr.'s time. All outsiders are relegated to the rank and file.

"I guess we just want to keep everything in the family. In-laws are fine, relatives also—look at Marissa, she's Benny's assistant. Nonrelatives are a completely different matter, they are not included," Narcisa believes.

Greg actualy had planned on professionalizing the company, but when he proposed it, Benny Sr. reportedly vetoed the idea.

"Perhaps because we don't see the need for it," offers Henrietta. "Simon used to say there are a lot of us. Look at how many we are and the next generation will be groomed for our positions."

Public Ownership Unresolved

Does the company have plans of going public?

"I don't know," Narcisa shrugs. "Nobody has ever said anything about it. But at the rate the company is going, maybe somebody has to do something. The ball is in my brother's court."

Indeed, and as we have seen, Benny Jr. is not the model employer his father was. A company burdened with such problems can barely think about the future; a situation signaling deterioration.

Family in Chaotic Business Functioning

From our preceding discussions, we can use Beavers Interactional Scales and summarize the functioning of the senior Gotong family, the family of Benny Jr., and that of Simon.

Senior Gotong's Family Functioning

1. *Structure of the family*
   a) Overt power: Moderate dominance, often chaotic
   b) Parental coalitions: Strong, but father dominant
   c) Closeness: Isolation, distancing behaviors, rivalry among siblings

2. *Mythology.* Generally incongruent (members have different views on the family)

3. *Goal-directed negotiation.* Poor

4. *Autonomy*
   a) Clarity of expression: Vague and hidden, overt and covert coercion
   b) Responsibility: Members sometimes take responsibility for individual actions, but also blames others or the culture
   c) Permeability: Generally unreceptive

5. *Family affect*
   a) Range of feelings: Some are expressed, others masked
   b) Mood and tone: Politeness without much warmth or affection with frequent bouts of hostility among siblings
   c) Unresolvable conflict: Definite conflict with sometimes severe impairment of group functioning
   d) Empathy: Marked absence of empathic responsiveness

6. *Global health-pathology scale.* Low borderline (8)

Benny Jr.'s Family Functioning

1. *Structure of the family*
   a)   Overt power: Marked dominance at times, often chaotic
   b)   Parental coalitions: Fair
   c)   Closeness: Distant, with isolation and distancing

2. *Mythology.* Somewhat incongruent (parents and children have different views of the family)

3. *Goal-directed negotiation.* Fair

4. *Autonomy*
   a)   Clarity of expression: Often vague and hidden
   b)   Responsibility: Members voice responsibility for own actions but also blame others
   c)   Permeability: Generally unreceptive

5. *Family affect*
   a)   Range of feelings: General masking of feelings especially by sons
   b)   Mood and tone: Depressed, ambivalent, striving for civility, fearful of overt conflict
   c)   Unresolvable conflict: Definite conflict with moderate impairment of group functioning
   d)   Empathy: Generally absent

6. *Global health-pathology scale.* High borderline (7)

Simon's Family Functioning

1. *Structure of the family*
   a) Overt power: Egalitarian
   b) Parental coalitions: Strong
   c) Closeness: Close with distant boundaries among members

2. *Mythology.* Generally congruent ("We should take care of each other.")

3. *Goal-directed negotiation.* Good

4. *Autonomy*
   a) Clarity of expression: Clear
   b) Responsibility: Members regularly take responsibility for individual actions
   c) Permeability: Consistently receptive

5. *Family affect*
   a) Range of feelings: Direct expression of a wide range of feelings
   b) Mood and tone: Usually affectionate, warm, humorous, optimistic
   c) Unresolvable conflict: Little unresolvable conflict

6. *Global health-pathology scale.* Optimal (2)

Narcisa puts her family at the low end of the midrange scale as shown by her responses on the SFI Health/Competence Subscale below.

Item	Narcisa
2	4
3	4
6	3
12	3
15	4
16	4
17	3
18 (R)	4
19 (R)	4
20	3
21	3
24 (R)	5
25 (R)	3
27 (R)	4
28	4
33	3
35	4
Sum	62
Classification	Midrange

The two sons of Benny Jr. agree that their family health is average, at most. Note the parallelism to the first-generation Gotong family. This seems to be an illustrative example of the oft-quoted principle in family systems: Family functioning patterns do get transmitted from one generation to the next unless deliberate efforts are designed to stop such transmission. The responses of Paolo and Alex on the <u>SFI Health/ Competence Subscale</u> are listed below.

Item	Paolo	Alex	Mean
2	3	3	3
3	3	3	3
4	3	3	3
6	4	4	4
12	3	3	3
15	4	3	3.5
16	4	3	3.5
17	3	3	3
18 (R)	3	3	3
19 (R)	3	3	3
20	4	3	3.5
21	3	3	3
24 (R)	1	1	1
25 (R)	3	3	3
27 (R)	3	3	3
28	3	3	3
33	3	3	3
35	3	3	3
Sum	56	53	54.5
Classification	Midrange	Midrange	Midrange

Simon's branch of the Gotong clan is satisfied with its family's health as shown by the responses of Henrietta, Michelle, and Annabel on the <u>SFI Health/Competence Subscale</u> below.

Item	Henrietta	Michelle	Annabel	Mean
2	2	2	2	2
3	1	2	1	1.3
4	2	2	2	2
6	1	1	1	1
12	1	1	1	1
15	2	2	2	2
16	2	2	3	2.3
17	2	1	1	1.3
18 (R)	1	1	1	1
19 (R)	2	2	2	2
20	1	1	1	1
21	1	2	1	1.3
24 (R)	1	1	1	1
25 (R)	1	1	1	1
27 (R)	2	2	2	2
28	2	1	2	1.7
33	2	1	1	1.3
35	1	1	1	1
36	3	3	3	3
Sum	30	29	29	29.3
Classification	Adequate	Adequate	Adequate	Adequate

Garments House business functioning can be rated as low midrange and on its way down, as can be gleaned from its detailed ratings on Dyer's (1986) checklist:

1. Family members are generally aware of their problems.

2. Family members have no definite plans for future needs, at least the plans which involve everyone.

3. Management succession has been coercive.

4. Ownership succession does not complement management succession.

5. The leader and possible successors have either a fair or chaotic relationship depending on the people involved.

6. Some relatives are being trained but the effectiveness of their training is questionable as decision-making is dominated by one person whose power is generally considered illegitimate.

7. Members of the firm do not share similar views on equity and competence.

8. Family members do not collaborate in solving problems.

9. Family members manage conflict poorly.

10. Family members do not trust each other much and neither do they trust their employees that much.

11. No outside feedback mechanisms exist.

12. Some members have a balanced perspective toward family and business while others do not.

III

THE FAMILY, THE BUSINESS

AN OLD CHINESE PROVERB GOES: The first generation starts the business, the second increases its wealth, and the third squanders it all.

There may be a grain of truth in that saying, because the five family corporations in this study have their problems. However, while some have fallen on the wayside, they are still surviving, thriving even, and thinking of expanding. Out of the five, only one company, Garments House, has third-generation family members helping out. The rest are mostly made up of the founder and the second-generation successors. Still, these five are a good enough mix and provide some interesting patterns of functioning.

Some of the patterns which surface in this work are unintended. In the course of analyzing data, some general discoveries emerge. Instead of ignoring them, we shall present them, offering possible explanations, while indicating need for further research in certain areas. Far from detracting from the significance of the study, these unintended findings are what make this work a truly exploratory one. Some patterns are also

197

Asian or even typically Filipino. Because of the paucity of local research on and by extension, local explanations for such behavior, it is difficult to contradict established Western management rules and postulate our own. Nevertheless, that is precisely what we will do here. The recommendations we shall make are, after all, empirically based.

Interesting and consistent patterns of functioning are discovered in both family and business realms. In analyzing each of the following variables, it may be helpful to keep in mind the diagram below.

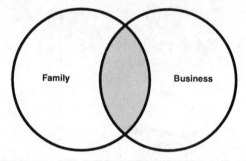

The shaded area accounts for a significant part in both spheres of family and business. Though we sometimes touch upon issues which differ (from those in the shaded area), we stress the findings in the shaded area.

Still, other variables have inevitably surfaced in the course of analyzing the data. However because of the constants of time and space, I suggest that they be examined more in depth in a follow-up study. Particularly worth pursuing are money and gender roles. Relevant questions may include: How does the family and each member view money? How do their views affect their relationship to money and each other? How does the family view the business? Is it their main source of income? How does their view or views affect the family business relationships?

How do husbands, wives, and children perceive and treat each other? How do these affect individual family members and the family as a whole? To what extent and on what bases are women accepted in the business? If not, why not? How does such practice affect the family firm?

Intergenerational problems is another significant topic for future study. Relevant questions are: Is there a "generation gap" in the family?

In what areas do the first and second, possibly even the third and the fourth generation of managers/owners not see eye-to-eye? What have given rise to these problems?

The findings from such a study would be helpful, I surmise, not only to those who study family dynamics but also to those interested in Filipino business behavior and management.

Let us now focus on the five families by comparing them to each other according to the variables of the present study.

Independence, Not Separation

All five families studied share similar patterns of individuation in both realms of family and business. Children who were allowed by their parents to mature at their own pace and make their own mistakes, learn to decide for themselves as they grow up. As parents, they have generally shown a similar tendency toward their offspring as regards the family business. This is apparent with the Hernandezes (Quality Shoes) and the Gochiamcos (Gochiamco Groceries, Inc.).

Those parents who extremely value family togetherness tend to fuss over their children and "overprotect" them, possibly restricting their growth. They show the same style in dealing with their now grown-up children in their businesses, ever reluctant to let the children make their own decisions, try out their own methods, much less rely on themselves. Such is the pattern in the Chua (Snackfood Delights) and Perez families (Excellence Printers). The children seem to be trying to search for their own identity without cutting ties with their parents. Such functional adaptation is exemplified by Helen (Snackfood Delights) in dealing with her father, and Peter and Paul (Excellence Printers) in dealing with their mother.

At the other end of the spectrum are those families where each one, for the most part, goes his or her own way. In Garments House, open disagreements and quarrels have erupted, sometimes across generations. The family and the business spheres have both suffered as a result.

Patterns of Individuation

All these businesses are successful financially, but the families run the gamut of enmeshment to disengagement. The individuation patterns of the five families and businesses are compared in this summary.

Individuated

- Gochiamco/Gochiamco Groceries, Inc.
- Hernandez/Quality Shoes

Enmeshed

- Chua/Snackfood Delights
- Perez/Excellence Printers

Disengaged

- Gotong/Garments House

Although it is difficult to generalize from just five case studies, we can discern certain patterns—families that are individuated, enmeshed, or disengaged.

Individuated Families

The families who seem to be successful in both the business and the family aspects are those who have mastered the balancing act: between too little care and smothering, between discipline and affection, between guidance and trust.

The Gochiamco brothers love and admire their parents, can stand on their own and rely on themselves (or each other) for decision-making, and have big plans for the future.

The Hernandez children emulate their mother's openness and credit her for their solidarity. They have even welcomed their stepsiblings (their father's children by another woman) into their own workplace.

They show that genuine forgiveness and concern can heal deep wounds, and generate satisfaction as well as peace of mind.

In the West, independence is highly priced. The pursuit of the American dream at all costs, the rugged individualism of brave pioneers, the often solitary path of the entrepreneur, the Fords who have built an empire at the expense of the family, the insistence on individual rights and privileges—all these have become enshrined in Western mythos. Perhaps that is only what it seems—a myth. Psychologists have expounded on individuation, and have concluded that it is not synonymous with independence as a prerequisite for a successful home-based, entrepreneurial business.

Our study shows that the most successful families (and individuals) are those who are individuated in the true sense of the word: independent yet close to one another. Respect for parents, care for siblings, and individual capabilities are not contradictory concepts, but rather complementary.

Discipline and fairness have been and are an integral part of child upbringing in these families. What is remarkable is that the children do not resent this and, in fact, are grateful for being brought up in such fashion. The results speak for themselves.

The Hernandez children, for instance, are well-mannered, mature, and respectful of their parents. Among the Gochiamcos, when one child gets punished, so does everybody else. The parents are perceived to be extremely fair, nevertheless. It is no wonder that in this family, the children say that they are raising their own kids in a similar manner.

On the business aspect, most of these families insist that all children get the same number of shares in their company, regardless of individual effort or time (as with the Gochiamcos), or according to amount of labor put in (as with the Hernandezes). Either way is perceived as fair by everybody involved.

This contradicts the notion held in the West, where individual rights and privileges above all else are heavily stressed. Cases of children bringing their parents to court or to the attention of a social worker because of a spanking abound. This would horrify Filipino parents who believe that a little discipline is necessary.

The caveat here is, (1) the one dispensing the discipline should be perceived as legitimate, and (2) the methods of discipline should be perceived as fair. When these two factors are established, the children accept discipline as natural.

The children in these families have been invariably exposed to the family business early on, but none of them have been forced into it. Some have been trained since childhood. The Gochiamco children, for instance, had to run errands for the grocery business during summer and Christmas vacations. The Hernandez children have had to help out whenever they could.

The common denominator here is the opportunity provided by the parents for the children to get involved in the business, yet have respected their children's own decisions and have not forced them into it. Remarkably enough, most of the children personally expressed the desire and did eventually join their family corporation.

While childhood exposure to the business also surfaces in Western family corporations, it is not deemed crucial by them. What Americans stress again and again is acquiring outside training such as studying for an MBA, working for a competitor prior to working in the family business, being trained by a nonrelative.

The five families studied show that early exposure is in fact significant. What can account for this contrary finding? Perhaps, children here are more sensitive, the vaunted Filipino (and Eastern—think of the Japanese!) capability of sensing covert rather than overt messages (currently termed emotional maturity). The children may imbibe (often unconsciously) the merits (and demerits) of working for the family, and decide to join the company later, based partly on those observations.

How about outside training? As studies of family corporations in the West show, it is important; however, our study shows it is not necessary.

In these families, the parents have never neglected their children even during the busiest periods of the business. Not surprisingly, all of them chose family over business without hesitation, when asked the hypothetical question, "If you were forced to choose between your family and your business, what would it be?"

This finding is certainly unexpected. In everyday lore, what we hear are people who have built empires at the expense of the family. Although management books have stressed again and again the importance of balancing these two spheres, the reality seems far from ideal. It is remarkable to have met three families in which the ideal is commonplace.

Spending long hours in the office, neglecting the family in the process, seems unnecessary. The excuse couched in this form: "But I am doing it for your [the family's] sake" cannot hold water anymore.

Perhaps cultural notions can again be used as a possible explanation. In the East, the family is highly prized, and much loving attention and care are given to making relationships work. Children, for the most part, are considered gifts from whatever deity they believe in.

The parents in these families revel in each other's company, and express their affection for each other. Tirso and Grace touch each other unabashedly. When he was still alive, Leon would send Conchita flowers every Valentine's day.

Again, this is a serendipitous discovery. It is indeed rare that Asian parents (especially Chinese) express their affection for each other openly. Perhaps this is just a peculiar characteristic of these three families, or can this be tied up somehow with individuation? For interestingly enough, the parents who do not express affection openly are either disengaged or too enmeshed. Perhaps they are too busy with their own professions to show affection openly, or one is very clearly dominant, that both are too embarrassed to show affection. I dare not insist on any generalization, however, for I do not personally believe that an open display of affection is crucial. Unlike in the West, where "you let it all hang out," in the Philippines, as in other Asian countries, cultural norms stress subtlety. Further research is needed, nevertheless.

The parents in these families are strong individuals with their own identity and interests. Tirso is a retired congressman. Leon has his close circle of friends. Because they have interests outside of the business, it has not been difficult for them to let go.

Their respective spouses are made from similar mold: it was Grace who started the venture; Conchita is the loyal wife and strong mother whom the children treat with respect.

It is quite surprising to find that the most successful individuals are those who have concerns outside the business. Common sense tells us that one factor for a successful company is the amount of effort and time the founder spends in it. How then can he or she nurture outside activities?

Yet, all these people do. In fact, they all deem community and social interests to be necessary. How do we account for this? The simplest explanation can just be that "all work and no play makes Pedro a dull businessman." Another explanation can be found in Covey's (1989) seventh habit: "sharpen the saw," or renew one's self. A more sophisticated imagery can be drawn from Maslow's famous work on self-actualized individuals: those who are well-rounded, those who have more than one pressing interest.

Decision-making is generally consensual. In Dyer's (1986) terms, these family companies have started out having a paternalistic culture (in a positive sense), but are on their way to becoming participative in nature.

The Gochiamco brothers consult with one another, and occasionally, with their parents. Miguel Hernandez is the designated leader, but he lets his siblings have a major part in decision-making.

This ties in generally with Western notions, though what is participative for Filipinos may still be deemed paternalistic by the Westerners. Be that as it may, it seems that moving toward democracy in business is significant to its success.

The subject "succession" is generally not taboo for discussion, because most of these families have been preparing or are already in the process of ensuring smooth transition to the next generation.

The Gochiamcos have drawn up plans, and Bosco even this early is thinking about the transfer to the third generation. The Hernandez children are the exception: Out of *delicadeza* (tact, refinement) and other personal reasons, they still have not faced the succession issue squarely. Enjoying the camaraderie of their extended family, it should prove no problem. Presently, everybody has an equal stake and the situation seems to be approved by all.

The frank discussion of transition is actually surprising because it goes contrary to stereotypical Filipino norms, where discussing the eventual death of the founder is considered *walang delicadeza* (tactless, lacks refinement). The families here are acting more in accordance with Western culture, where wills and lawyers are a normal part of the process.

The Beavers SFI Style score, however, cannot be adopted as it is in the Filipino context. All the five families scored in the moderate centripetal range. However, the interviews and responses on the other subscales prove otherwise. In other words, although the members tended to depend on the family for their satisfaction (as far as the Beavers SFI Style score is concerned), the result of the interviews and the other subscales contradict this finding. What could account for this discrepancy?

It could be that items 4, 14, and 27 (determining style in the SFI Style score) are misinterpreted by the respondents. Although the last two items ("we argue a lot and never solve problems" and "our family members would rather do things with other people than together") seem unambiguous enough, item number 4 ("the grownups in this family understand and agree on family decisions") may easily be misintepreted. Item number 4, for instance, can be taken to mean that parents respect each other and make decisions consensually. Or it may mean that one is dominant over the other in an authoritarian decision-making style, with the submissive parent always acquiescing. Therefore, these items, especially the scores assigned to them, should be reworked so as to reflect what they indeed need to measure and show.

Enmeshed Families

Let us now discuss the still enmeshed ones, some of whom are struggling toward individuation.

Those families who are enmeshed generally still lead harmonious lives. The children adore their parents and vice-versa. Communication seems to be no problem at most times, and the children are all encouraged to speak out, almost without fear of being rejected or misunderstood. Helen, the apple of her parents' eye, admits to reveling in the family solidarity. Peter, and to some extent, Paul Perez, admire their parents for taking time out to help them even when they are very busy.

The parents in these families are extremely close to each other. The Chuas still give each other gifts. The Perezes have genuine heartfelt concern for each other. Nora's greatest fear is that her husband will have another heart attack, and has prevailed on him to retire from the business.

The parents generally have their own interests, though one usually gives in to the other. Nora gives in to Jacinto and vice-versa to keep the peace. Cecile has her own insurance concern, but does not neglect her husband and daughter.

It is in their business that these families encounter problems. The parents have generally tended to smother the children rather than set them free. Although this may be acceptable in the family, this remains a contentious issue in their business. Helen is disappointed when her father treats her like his little girl, even if she feels herself to be capable. The father seems unable to allow her to make decisions without interfering. She is struggling toward individuation. Nora Perez admits that her one mistake may have been not giving her sons enough training in business while they were young and making things too easy for them. She feels her sons are not capable enough, a view the sons privately but never openly disagree with.

None of these children have been formally trained in the business. None have been forced into it either. This is unfortunate, as both the Chua and the Perez families are having difficulties with transitions.

Following Dyer (1986), we can say that company culture is either paternalistic or professional. In Snackfood Delights and Excellence Printers, the founders have a strong hand in the business, and are mostly obeyed by either their spouses or outsiders. Children are generally not trusted enough to make major decisions.

The succession issue is being addressed but both families are entertaining the thought of bringing in more outsiders, if the children are not capable of ensuring continuity of the business. The Perez family wants to go public someday, while the Chua family already has nonfamily members in its stockholders' board.

Parents obviously value closeness, with children acknowledging its advantages but at the same time desiring more freedom. Still, the averages on the SFI subscale are mostly in the adequate range, which shows great hope that parents and children are capable of transcending differences and working things out. Their SFI Style scores are rated as centripetal, i.e., centered on family.

Disengaged Families

These families who adopt a more distant style generally do not have satisfactory personal lives. Because of parental absence, children have acted out in several ways, most of them negatively. The relationships among the Gotong siblings leave much to be desired.

Pacita appears to have been responsible for the upbringing of her children, but she is not strong enough to counter the rifts developing among them. Her husband, though loving toward her, is distant to the children. He expects excellent scholastic performance and when they succeed, rewards them with material gifts, but not with his presence, which the children admit they yearned for.

None of the children in these families have been trained in the business and have had only minimal exposure. The Gotong children were busy with schoolwork, even taking advanced classes during summer breaks.

In the disengaged families, the parents cannot trust their children to be valid successors. Benny Gotong Sr. passed away without appointing an heir, and Garments House is now in crisis. Relationships among the children are fair at best, but generally poor. The Gotongs may still fight it out in court: There is a clear picture of dissatisfaction experienced by some. Cohesion is not strong and expressiveness is not encouraged for fear of being disinherited or accused of disobedience and disrespectfulness.

Following Beavers and Hampson (1990), their styles are still classified as centripetal. However, I would prefer to think of them more as centrifugal—at least in the Filipino context. (I feel that the SFI Style Subscale here is not applicable to us locally, and we should validate it more before using it for further research.)

Achieving Individuation

We have seen how individuation patterns surface and become almost automatic in both the family and business. We have identified the most successful families in both fields—those who are fully individuated, close yet not too close, so to speak. For those who have not yet achieved this ideal, undergoing family systems therapy may be beneficial.

Family Therapy for Individuation

Will family therapy be more effective than individual therapy for Filipino families? I believe so. Jung (1984, 371) makes an observation about Chinese families, which applies equally well to our context:

> To serve traditional Chinese in individual therapy is, in some respects, contrary to Chinese cultural values. Individual growth and development are not within the accepted norm of the Chinese culture, for the individual is always responsible to the past, present or future . . . since the Chinese cannot perceive the individual aside from his family, it is the family, *not the individual*, [emphasis mine] that must be involved in therapy.

The distorted relationship patterns displayed in some of these families, according to Bowen (1978), have different effects, but generally have a prime cause: the lack of differentiation of self, which is inextricably tied up with latent or overt family anxiety. How does Bowen recommend therapy to proceed? Generally, it begins with a family evaluation, with focus on the presenting problem: Who has the symptom, when and where it originated, what developed, what has been the family response? Family history is then examined over in great detail with focus on three variables—differentiation, intensity of anxiety in the system, and mechanisms to bind anxiety.

Another effective approach may be that espoused by Minuchin (1978), who with his structural family therapy, gives the therapist an important yet noncentral role. Through several steps—actualizing family transactional patterns, marking boundaries, escalating stress, assigning tasks, making use of symptoms, manipulating the mood of the family, giving nurturance, providing education and guidance (Hansen and L'Abate 1982)—the therapist hopes to bring the family into a better balance between enmeshment and disengagement.

Pointers for Individuation

From our study of the five family businesses, what can we recommend for families who want to succeed in both business and personal lives in terms of individuation? They all flow from our previous analyses. Here are some suggestions based on our findings.

Balance family togetherness, neither too much nor too little. Establish each one's public and private boundaries.

It is better for the founders to pursue their own interests outside of the family business and to encourage their spouses to have their own as well. However, stay attuned to each other and show affection.

Do not sacrifice family interests for business' sake. Rossenblatt (1985) suggests: Use time flexibly, make time budgets and stick to them, adjust priorities, and learn to delegate.

Encourage early exposure of children to the business, but do not force them into it. Discipline is important, but so is affection. When disciplining the children, ensure that methods are perceived as fair. Allow the children to make their own choices (but the parents should still be there for support). As much as possible, strive to proceed from a paternalistic to a participative style in decision-making. Mancuso and Shulman (1981, 28) urge:

> Let the kids make mistakes. A powerful parent often dominates the business and the family until the children are reluctant to compete. The problem is compounded when what little authority they may have gained is snatched back after a minor mistake or two.

The children are not absolved of responsibility, either. They should strive to be honest with themselves about why they are entering the business.

Discuss the succession issue with everyone involved. Rosenblatt (1985, 195) suggests that daughters be counted as possible successors, that they be given "appropriate education and opportunity to learn about the job."

Unlike the Westerners, we Filipinos do not value extreme independence. As we have seen, in both family and business, the successful ones uphold the virtues of family togetherness and stability. Yet they have learned to respect and give each other enough space to grow.

When Power Is Clear and Acknowledged

Patterns of power vary among the families. In one type, the power holders are the same for both the family and business arenas: Jacinto, the father of the Perezes and founder of Excellence Printers; Emilio, the father of Helen Chua and founder of Snackfood Delights.

In another, power is overtly or tacitly apportioned between family and business, as in the case of the Hernandezes: the father, Leon, in business; the mother, Conchita, at home. The Gochiamcos have acted in the same manner, but in reverse: the father Tirso in the house, the mother Grace in the office.

Whether power is the same or different for the family and the business, it is clear and acknowledged by most of the clan members. In one case, though, authority lines are not as marked, resulting in a laissez-faire and often chaotic home atmosphere as mirrored in the Gotong family. The father minds the store while the mother, the house, but she, apparently, is not strong enough to prevent cracks in the family unity. Perhaps because of a submissive personality or cultural factors, Pacita relinquished power readily to her eldest son when her husband passed away. The reverberations are still being felt to this day: a sister estranged, a son-in-law ousted after a bitter struggle, tears, and threats of court litigation.

Patterns of Power

Power patterns for the five cases are summarized below.

Same power holder in family and business

- Emilio Chua/Snackfood Delights
- Jacinto Perez/Excellence Printers

Division of authority between family and business

- Leon and Conchita Hernandez/Quality Shoes
- Tirso and Grace Gochiamco/Gochiamco Groceries, Inc.

Ambivalent power structure in family

- Gotong/Garments House

Power in One Person

The first type is where power is exercised clearly by the same person in the family and the business. If the prevalent leadership style is egalitarian, then everyone seems content both in their personal and professional lives. If the prevalent leadership style is marked by traces of dominance, then the family members can remain close, care for each other, and look out for one another. However, the business may suffer.

An example is the Perez family. Jacinto admits that neither of his two sons seems ready to handle the business on his own, making it difficult for the couple to retire permanently. Having exercised moderate control over their sons at home, they have followed the same pattern in the business. Their sons have, so far, been limited to minor decision-making and still have to consult with their parents often. The Perez couple recognize this shortcoming, though, and state that they are trying to make their sons more confident and capable.

Not so with Emilio. Having pampered his only child at home, he continues to "treat her like a little girl" and remains the sole authority in the business. Family life is relatively harmonious, with Helen still professing great affection for her father. However, she is often disappointed in the office, but to her credit, continues to inform her father of her feelings. Attached to the highly successful snackfood company he started, Emilio seems unable to let go.

How do we account for this dichotomy? Asian norms of filial piety and obedience can be taken to mean that authoritarian leadership is in fact legitimate and natural. Children raised in such families do not necessarily rebel, especially if their parents are perfectly loving and genuinely care for them. Still, the business sphere is different: What works for the home in this case may not necessarily work for the office. When filial obedience clashes with educational or societal norms (e.g., getting an MBA abroad or working for a multinational first), conflict invariably ensues. This conflict, though, is a lot more muted than that in the West where full-blown quarrels easily erupt over perceived encroachments of territorial rights.

There seems to be a relationship between individuation and power such that if the family is individuated, power tends to be more egalitarian. In the Perez and Chua families, the family style has been classified previously as more enmeshed. With individuation still to be achieved and power centralized, great care should be taken to make the transition process acceptable to all without open or passive opposition by the dominated ones.

As for insider views of the family, SFI scores on the Leadership Subscale are in the optimal and adequate ranges. This implies that delegation of power is clear and considered legitimate by everyone. These factors are also mirrored in the other types. Let us turn to the second one, where power is divided between family and business.

Power Divided Family and Business

If the prevalent leadership style is egalitarian, then the family is successful, and so is the business. The Gochiamco children know who makes the final decisions in both spheres, and because the division of power is perceived as perfectly legitimate, highly proper even, everyone is content. With her sources of power based on legitimacy, expertise, and reward, Grace has ensured a smooth transition to her two sons, who share authority in their own way. Tirso has similar bases of authority: information and charisma. Both Tirso and Grace employ coercive methods at times, but with the children judging such techniques as perfectly fair, only few problems arise. Besides, their children view them as their best role models.

Such is also the case with Conchita and her clan. She and Leon are basically egalitarian in exercising authority, earning the respect, affection, and, in Conchita's case, admiration and awe from the children. With his expert skills, and by virtue of his being the founder, Leon was the acknowledged power in the business, but he trained his sons well. Succession to the three eldest was smooth, and the same happened the second time, with the fourth son Miguel assigned at the helm. As for Conchita, she is the mother everyone idolizes. With great strength and tenderness, she brought up her own children, and accepted her stepchildren as well, both of whom are highly attached to her. Her authority is legitimate and referent. Rarely does she have to resort to reward and punishment.

Where power is clear and dispensed with democratically, individuation often results. It is illuminating to note that these two families also scored high on the individuation area. Both are able to balance togetherness and distantiation effectively. Succession has proven to be smooth so far. Perhaps that is why Miguel is not yet thinking seriously about his turn.

Most of the succession cases have been successful, partly because the founders have other "things to attend to after retirement." They see stopping work not as a cessation or an affront to their personal identity, but as a chance to do other things.

SFI scores on the family are mostly in the optimal and the adequate ranges.

Unbalanced Power

In the third type, power is not balanced between family and business. If power is minimal in the family and exercised only moderately in the business, the conflicts in the family can spill out into the business, at the expense of both. An illustrative example of this is the Gotong clan.

Because Pacita's influence is weak, and the eldest son quite used to getting his way, the original founder (who could have been a mediator) out of the picture, chaos results. When no one knows who is in power, or the one who has seized it is perceived to have done so illegitimately, struggles inevitably arise. Add to this scenario the dethroning of an acknowledged more capable successor, and further confusion reigns. Among all the five families analyzed in this study, Garments House has the worst problems with transitions.

As for insider views of the family, SFI scores on the Leadership Subscale here are mostly in the midrange and borderline areas.

We have seen how the power issue can affect the effectiveness of the family, and sometimes, of the business as well. What can be done?

Dealing with Power and Authority

Family therapy may be essential to those whose home lives are chaotic, where authority is unrecognized.

A prime need of children, especially during the growing-up years, is a sense of trust, which can dissipate when no one seems to be in control. Left to their own devices, they may, if lucky or born with some inner strength, turn out all right. More often than not, however, they go astray in one form or the other, resulting in poor relationships with their parents, their siblings, their peers, and other authority figures—most likely in school.

Family Therapy for Power

Haley (1976) would conduct therapy along power lines, but he would not assert himself too much as a therapist. Drawing from extensive research with families of delinquents and schizophrenics (the most extreme of distorted power issues), Haley considers communication as paramount, and the family of origin is an important "training ground."

How do we deal with too much power? Holding on for too long is linked with individuation. It follows that therapy would be similar to the strategies applicable to individuation. Rosenblatt (1985) elaborates on this yet again:

> In business-operating families, the way offspring-parent relationships operate often makes business decisions a source of tension. Contributing to the problems are . . . confusion over who does what and problems created by the carryover of roles from family life to business life and vice-versa. Added to this is, no doubt, the need for offspring to differentiate (individuate) themselves from parents, to know and to show that they can function autonomously, that they are not merely dependent puppies whose business role has been granted purely on a kinship basis. For a parent, the offspring's interest in individuation in the decision area may be threatening. Offspring who individuate by disagreeing with a parent on a decision may seem to the parent to discount the parent's accumulated business sense and previous success. Disagreement may even suggest to the parent that the offspring would like the parent out of the way.

Toward Smooth Succession

As we have discussed, succession is also tied up closely with the power issue. The power holder as well as the would-be successor play major roles in the successful resolution of the succession issues. Here are some practical recommendations for ensuring smooth succession in the business.

Ensure that authority is clear-cut, whether it rests solely on an individual or shared by a number of individuals. Though moderate dominance may work oftentimes, an egalitarian leadership seems the most effective as the families studied have shown. Working toward the individuation of everyone involved is necessary.

Identify and educate at least one possible successor, and make that choice clear to the rest. The chosen one "needs chances to perform and make mistakes in an executive role, needs supportive supervision, needs to be respected as an individual, and does not need to be indulged" (Rosenblatt 1985, 188). Although many Western management books recommend training by a nonrelative, we have seen how effective training by an informed, egalitarian parent can be. In the Philippine context, learning from and working with a loved one rather than an outsider may prove even more fruitful.

The person stepping down must learn to genuinely delegate authority, and even be willing to work out a good plan with the parties concerned. At the same time, he or she should be open to the idea that the chosen successor may not live up to his or her ideals. In this case, it may be wise to have alternate succession plans ready. Discussing succession may sometimes be difficult because of societal norms. Lansberg (1983, 9) has noted:

> The norms regulating behavior of family members discourage parents and offspring from discussing the future of the family beyond the lifetime of the parents. This is particularly true to discussions of economic and financial matters, which are often viewed as a branch of etiquette or as denoting a lack of mutual trust. These norms function to ensure that relationships within the family are guided by personal caring, rather than ulterior motives such as economic self-interest.

All well and good, but future problems may arise.

The power holder needs to acquire other interests other than the business. With his or her identity not exclusively anchored to the firm, he or she can find it easier, sometimes even a relief, to let go. To paraphrase an old proverb, old age and retirement need not be a winter, but a fruitful harvest.

As for the successors, they should be sensitive to their parents' pain of letting go. They should balance assertiveness with respect, care, show affection, ensuring that the transition is in the best interest of all involved. They can take to heart Covey's (1989) fourth and fifth dicta: Think win/win. And seek first to understand, then to be understood.

Quality of Relationships and Alliances

Recall that there are three basic relationships within the nuclear family: spouse-spouse, parent-child, and sibling-sibling. The interactions among them provide some interesting patterns. The table below groups the five families accordingly.

Family/ Business	Marital Alliance	Parent- Child	Sibling Relationships
Gochiamco/ Gochiamco Groceries, Inc.	Strong	Consistent, perceived as fair	Good
Hernandez/ Quality Shoes	Fair to good	Consistent, perceived as fair	Good
Perez/ Excellence Printers	Strong	Perceived traces of inequity by mother	Fair
Gotong/ Garments House	Strong	Preferential treatment by parents	Poor
Chua/ Snackfood Delights	Strong	NA (Helen Chua is an only child.)	NA (Helen Chua is an only child.)

Sibling Relationships

The quality of sibling relationships can be classified into (1) excellent, (2) generally fair, and (3) relatively poor. Let us first examine the groups where siblings display excellent relationships.

Excellent Sibling Relationships

There are two types of this relationship: (1) when the parental bond is cohesive, and where the children perceive sibling treatment as equitable; and (2) where the parental bond is fair at best, but sibling treatment is nevertheless perceived as fair.

Examples of the first are the Gochiamcos, the second, the Hernandezes. It seems here that the deciding factor is the treatment of children. Schvaneveldt and Ihinger (1979, 462) put it this way: "When parents approach an arbitration situation with consistency and congruence according to justice norms which have been clearly articulated, there will be less conflict interaction between siblings."

Generally, family functioning is healthy in all these cases. If marital alliances are cohesive and parents' treatment perceived as fair, then sibling relationships tend to be good. Because there are no favorites, brothers and sisters can learn to trust each other without any hidden agenda. They care for each other and try to settle disputes in a consensual fashion.

The children learn to trust against the background of a stable parental bond, and learn to take care of one another as well. Tattling and keeping secrets do not work, and children soon have to resort to more positive ways of relating. As Caplow (1968, 99) explains:

> When the parental coalition is so solid that no child is ever allowed to form a winning coalition with one parent against the other, we may expect to see strong coalitions among the children, and even a condition of general solidarity uniting all the children of a large family.

Balancing normally emerges as an important sibling function. In relating to their parents, they try to balance the close alliance of their parents with their own strong ties. Is this surprising? No, for balancing here is positive: The siblings support each other, and do not try to gain parental attention by tattling or colluding against one another.

When the marital relationship is cohesive, it is stable enough to ensure a diffusion of power. Though there is always a power holder (as discussed in the previous section), he or she is accorded respect and legitimacy, and leadership style in turn tends to be egalitarian in most.

In the business aspect, the situation is as healthy as that in the family. A strong and loving marital alliance goes a long way in ensuring the effectiveness of the firm. Gochiamco Groceries, Inc. and Quality Shoes are both planning to expand. This gives even more credence to what seems to emerge from the findings: A healthy family usually ensures a healthy business.

Sibling functions hinge mostly on mutual regulation and direct services. They do not need to resort to coercive or even reward tactics. Just as they helped each other during schooldays, siblings cooperate and work together in the business.

Normally, siblings have an equitable division of labor, with their own responsibilities and influence, as with Boy and Bosco Gochiamco, and the Hernandez children and stepchildren. In these two cases the underlying factor is the legitimacy of the leadership structure.

Recall that an egalitarian power structure is seen to be optimal. This is so especially during times of transition when parents want their offspring to take over.

How about the power structure among the children themselves? Unless all are equally capable and experienced, it is not practical to insist on an equal division of responsibility. Too many cooks may literally spoil the broth, as it has several times in Western case studies.

In the Philippines, the kuya or the ate is treated with respect at home, and in these successful families, they are also treated similarly in the office. This makes for a more tranquil workplace, and as long as the elder siblings exercise power judiciously and train the younger ones to take their place later on (as exemplified by the Hernandezes), this may in fact be optimal.

Succession and inheritance are not sensitive issues and usually have been discussed. Future plans have been, or are being, threshed out. In most cases, shares in the company are divided equally among all siblings. (Though succession has not been thoroughly discussed by the Hernandezes, no problem is foreseen.)

Where the marriage bond is strong or fairly cohesive, treatment of family members perceived as fair, power structure egalitarian, then individuation is almost always achieved. Such is the case with the Gochiamcos and the Hernandezes.

Conflict management is virtually an art form with SFI scores on the Conflict Subscale in the optimal or adequate ranges. The siblings usually hold family discussions, where the ideas and sentiments of each are voiced and discussed.

Generally Fair Sibling Relationships

How about families where sibling interactions are fair most of the time, but deteriorate during times of crisis? Here, we come across an interesting factor—the marriage bond may either be strong or only fair, but the deciding point appears again to be the perceived treatment of children. In the Perezes's case, Paul believes that his parents prefer Peter over him (though they may deny this).

Family functioning is fair at best. Most members agree that they get along well enough most of the time. When problems crop up, however, resentments are revealed and conflicting triangles may form.

For the Perezes, no parent is dominating; in fact, Jacinto's leadership style is generally egalitarian. Yet, to some extent, he (and especially Nora) seem to look at their eldest, Peter, more as the "good boy." Paul and Peter both admit they are closer to their younger siblings than to each other.

Differentiation is one dominant sibling function. The Perez children have different personalities. Perhaps, to get attention and differentiate himself from his brother Peter, Paul acts more aggressively as compared to his "soft" sibling.

The business sphere seems to mirror family relationships. Whatever arguments Peter and Paul may have can be settled by the mother who always has the final say, but not without their resentment.

In the business, siblings may have their own duties and responsibilities, but they tend to overlap, treading on each other's boundaries. Peter and Paul argue about production and marketing (although this is a factor independent from their personal relationships, and is tied up with the nature of the divisions themselves).

Succession and inheritance issues are still up in the air. The Perezes do not feel that any of their sons can manage the business as yet, and are thinking of dividing the company or going professional.

Individuation among the Perez children has not been fully achieved; they are still enmeshed. Conflict management is only fair, and may deteriorate when the parents are no longer in the picture. SFI scores of all the children are only in the lower end of the adequate range.

Relatively Poor Sibling Relationships

We now go into families where sibling relationships are relatively poor. Once more, the crucial factor seems not to be the marriage bond: the Gotong couple seems to be loving enough (but we have to keep in mind that the wife defers to her husband most of the time). What is common among these families is that the children perceive their parents to be playing favorites without legitimate basis. As a result, family functioning is chaotic, marked by collusions between parent and child, and among siblings themselves.

Among the Gotongs, relationships are weak. Both parents favor the eldest son, to the fury of the youngest daughter Narcisa, who tries to differentiate by being "more assertive." Ihinger (1975) believes that as children mature and are exposed to outside concepts of justice, they tend to challenge family (and even clan) equity norms. Narcisa is born Chinese, but is raised in the Philippines where women are not necessarily excluded because of gender. She believes the Chinese custom to be extremely prejudicial to women.

There are no triangles but, because the parents are allied with each other, two-way alliances predominate: Narcisa and Simon, at times, though Simon prefers to play the role of mediator. According to Zuk (1972), when their other siblings have marked, clearly defined, and dominant roles, the others would tend to act as the go-between.

The predominant sibling function is differentiation with the other more positive roles (such as mutual regulation or day-to-day services) nearly absent. The siblings apparently devote a lot of their time and energy trying to compete with each other, such as in the case of Narcisa and Benny Jr. In the process, the business suffers as well. The bitter rivalry between Narcisa and her brother was exacerbated by the ouster of her husband from the company.

Benny Jr. dominates the business but his authority is not recognized by the others. Succession and inheritance are sensitive issues and power struggles are usually bitter. The Gotongs "solved" this problem by getting Narcisa and her husband to leave, and compromised by allowing them to retain their shares. In terms of individuation, the children are too disengaged at this point.

Conflict management is poor, usually characterized by collusions and coercion. SFI scores on the Conflict Subscale tend to be at midrange with some in the borderline altogether. For the sole case involving an only child, a strong marital coalition means that the child cannot play off one parent against the other. Helen Chua confides that she has tried, but has never succeeded.

Alliances and Conflict Management

Because this section is tied up with individuation and power, the recommendations outlined in the preceding sections are valid here. We stress a point made earlier: The level of anxiety affects the level of fusion and differentiation in a system.

Therapy for Conflict Management

Although diffusing the anxiety (e.g., stopping a crisis) may solve the immediate problem, the long-term solution is still the arduous road to differentiation. This should be kept in mind while working with triangle situations.

Bowen (1976) uses a special technique for dealing with triangles: the therapist himself tries to get in and triangulate without falling into the trap, so to speak, while still relating effectively with the other two. Bowen believes that this sort of modelling can be useful and insists that he has employed the tactic at various times with apparent success.

Building Effective Alliances

When the family system is functional, then relationships in the business generally work themselves out. However, to make alliances and conflict management more effective in this setting, the following suggestions are made for the parents/founders.

Ensure that the marital alliance is as strong and consistent as possible. Wives should also be given consideration because the most successful businesses are those in which the wife is supportive (of the husband) either actively or passively. As Danco (1981, 43) says, "We are not women behind the men. We are the women with the men." Therefore, decisions should be agreed upon by the couple and communicated clearly to the children. This prevents one child or another from trying to collude with either parent to the detriment of the whole system.

The notion of fairness should be a reality, not just an ideal to be desired. Within the home, fairness is usually synonymous with equality. In the business, fairness is usually based on clearly-seen and clearly-defined merit system backed by rules plain for everyone to see. "Fairness does not lie in equality. It doesn't lie in the intent of the giver. Over and over again, I have seen that what is fair is only that which is accepted by all parties as fair" (Danco 1979, 200).

Mancuso and Shulman (1991, 77) caution, "Don't become obsessed with being [equal] in handing out management positions to family members. Simply because one qualified sibling earns a key management position does not dictate that other, less qualified family members be equally recognized."

As much as possible, make division of labor clear among children. Mancuso and Shulman (28) even suggest keeping an organizational chart so "people will know where they stand." This helps diffuse power and also helps prevent accusations of inequity especially when dealing with promotion or succession. Try separating ownership from management. It may probably be a realistic solution to problems such as an incompetent relative working in the firm.

Do not impose tasks on the children but assign tasks that will help them individuate. They will tend to gravitate to the responsibilities their different personalities and interests lead them to. In case there is conflict, either parent has to step in and discuss the matter thoroughly with all involved parties. Usually, a compromise satisfactory to all can be reached. If sibling relationships are excellent, this problem need not arise in the first place. Siblings will naturally support each other or work things out effectively (in their own fashion, the way they usually do.)

Try to go beyond cultural norms such as those based on gender, particularly when dealing with children in the business. Hidden resentments can sabotage relationships on all sides. Have a genuine, open dialogue.

Parents should be coaches and teachers, a role many entrepreneurs may find difficult. They cannot expect their children to know how to handle the business without guidance. As Danco (1979, 145) puts it:

> For the founder, the duty to teach his successors increases with every passing year, but that duty doesn't necessarily bring with it the ability to teach well. A true teacher plants seeds in what he hopes is fertile soil, seeds which then sprout and grow in their own way with only as much of his help as is absolutely necessary.

As we have noted in the section on individuation, outside training may be important (e.g., getting an MBA, working for another company), but not necessary. There have been successful transitions even when the children went to work for their parents right after college. In this regard, one effective early exposure the children can have is parents discussing business (over the dinner table) especially in a positive manner. Refrain from griping about business troubles; instead, rear them up with tales of a vision, a dream, and all the rewards that come from having a family company.

If parents still do not know whom to choose as the designated successor, they can try developing an "executive team" composed of all eligibles. This team can then be given a certain task. Another strategy may be to divide the business into several smaller ones and give one to each sibling, ensuring that it will suit their interests, and in the process, lead them to develop their capabilities all the more. Spin-off may work or a new adventure can be started altogether. Of course, professional management can always be an option.

Brothers and sisters should genuinely try to listen to one another. Communication, here and elsewhere, is significant. An open, nondefensive stance is the best. Siblings should always be aware that in their business relationships, they may sometimes "recapitulate ancient rivalries, and . . . psychological pressures" on each other (Levinson 1971, 97). This is easier said than done, however, and Levinson empathizes:

> Since there is love and hate in all relationships, theirs cannot, by definition, be pure. They should not feel guilty about their anger with each other, but they do need to talk it out. Having done that, they then must consider how they can divide the tasks in the organization so that each will have a chance to acquire and demonstrate competence and work in a complementary relationship with the other.

Although one sibling may have been dominant in the family context, this may not work well in the business unless the others acknowledge it as legitimate. Especially in business, things should be clear. Recall that in successful families and businesses, sibling functions include balance, mutual regulation, and direct services. These are consequences of the quality of sibling relationships.

Work well and work with love. The business started as the outgrowth of someone's dream and was nurtured by him or her. For the family business is not just any job, it is more, yes, a labor of love. The successors should keep that in mind when their time comes.

In-Laws and Other Extended Family Members

All the families interviewed either accepted or said they would accept in-laws into their family circle albeit in varying degrees. The level of cohesiveness or disengagement of families seems to have a positive correlation with their reaction to in-laws.

Acceptance in the Family

Those who have individuated fully and whose sibling alliances are cohesive welcome in-laws with affection, viewing them as additional members of the family rather than as threats. The Hernandezes and the Gochiamcos illustrate this.

Those families with one member or another who still has to differentiate from the rest, and where one parent or the other has difficulty letting go, will generally accept in-laws as long as they conform with the family's expectations.

Nora Perez wanted to choose a wife for her son until her husband put his foot down. Emilio Chua would veto many of his daughter's suitors, deeming none good enough for her.

Families who are mainly disengaged from each other would treat the entry of in-laws the way they normally do—with passive acceptance. The Gotongs fall into this category.

Acceptance in the Business

Applied to business, though, things are not as clear-cut. In some cases, even where in-laws are loved and cared for by the family, it is deemed more advisable to leave them out of the firm. The Gochiamcos used a Chinese parable to justify their relegating a sister-in-law to "sitting in the board without voting power."

In some families, in-laws are accepted into the business only if they displayed competence, not just willingness. The Perezes had to request a daughter-in-law to leave because she was not doing well in her position.

When in-laws have proven themselves competent, however, their participation in the business is generally welcomed, and they have even been made to assume big responsibilities.

The Hernandezes all agreed that should any of their spouses want to join the firm, in-laws would be very much welcome and would be eligible for senior management should they prove worthy.

The entry of an in-law into the firm, however, does not automatically make him or her an eligible successor. A potent display of capability (without stepping on anyone's toes) may help. This in-law will normally be put as head of management with the original children of the founder comprising the rest of the board. Emilio Chua may designate an in-law as heir if he could prove himself, but will always provide a place for his daughter in the board. In case in-laws prove to be no problem, a deciding factor may be the level of trust given them by the founder.

A common function for in-laws seems to be training the founder's children. This seems to be a compromise between the Western insistence on outside training and the Eastern penchant for training within the firm itself. An in-law can be more objective than the parent and the child does not have to go outside to be trained for a firm he or she will eventually work for anyway.

An advantage in-laws provide is objectivity. Less caught up in the emotional entanglement of the original family, they can even be a bridge. When the Gochiamco brothers quarreled, it was the wife of one of them who urged reconciliation. Because the sibling ties are strong, peace was readily restored.

On the other side of the coin, when will the entry of in-laws into the business prove unwise? If sibling relationships are chaotic to begin with, then the entry of in-laws might make matters worse. Such is the situation in the Gotong clan—a brother-sister rivalry went from sibling competitiveness to a raging battle for corporate control with an in-law complicating the picture. Mancuso and Shulman (1991, 38) put it picturesquely: "A son- or a daughter-in-law can serve as a lightning rod for family hostility."

In-law relationships among the five families are summarized below.

> **In-laws accepted in family and business (if capable and willing)**
> - Henry Lim Sr./Garments House
> - Hernandezes/Quality Shoes—if they decide to join
>
> **In-laws accepted in family, but in business, with some reservations (only if capable and "do not cause trouble")**
> - Mary Gochiamco/Gochiamco Groceries, Inc.
> - Grace and Rita, initially Perez/Excellence Printers
>
> **No in-laws yet, but will be accepted in family and business (if capable and willing)**
> - Chua/Snackfood Delights

Family Network Intervention Therapy

Divorced from the outside world, the nuclear family cannot exist effectively. Considering dysfunctional relationships with in-laws and other relatives, family therapy should take a broader view. It has only been recently that attempts to incorporate "outsiders" into the treatment have been made. The family network intervention of Speck and Attneave (1973), Rueveni (1979), and others is one good example.

Drawing from the concept of zones, these network therapists generally intend to improve communication and relationships among members of the basic family and their significant others—relatives and friends. Rueveni (1979) lists five specific goals: (1) facilitating rapid connections; (2) encouraging the sharing of problems with the immediate family; (3) facilitating communication; (4) exploring difficulties on a deeper level; and (5) assisting in the formation of support groups.

Usually, therapy takes place in stages, from retribalization to polarization, then mobilization to breakthrough, exhaustion, and finally, elation (Speck and Attneave 1973). The therapist has to be empathetic and skillful for he or she may be called upon to play several network roles as convenor, mobilizer, choreographer, resource consultant, strategist, and so on (Rueveni 1979). If deemed capable, family members themselves can be asked to take on some of these roles.

How effective has family network intervention been? There seems to be a less theoretical basis for this, and therapy is definitely tedious, leaving many participants exhausted. Still, with in-laws and others, it may prove to be the most effective. Hansen and L'Abate (1982, 277) remark, "Although there is no comparative research, case studies report good success. The success is not expressed as 'they lived happily ever after' but rather that realistic coping has been achieved."

Building Smooth Business Relationships with In-Laws

For in-laws who want to enter the family business, here are some tips: Tread carefully and respect family norms. You have married into the family but not necessarily into the business. Do not expect preferential treatment in both spheres. Prove your capability. Do not bank on your familial ties to merit approval in the business. Be aware that if sibling relationships are chaotic or even hostile, a meddling in-law may make things worse. Avoid, as much as possible, engaging in conflict which have taken root long before you came into the scene. (Of course, this is easier said than done!)

If you are the founder or a member of the founder's clan, be aware of the anxieties in-laws face (e.g., as outsiders coming into a tight-knit family) and treat them with consideration. Give them a chance to prove themselves. Negotiate a suitable time frame, and set objective measures of performance. Do not reward them solely because of their relationships with your own children. Bear in mind the advantages of having in-laws: potentially, they can be trainors, referees, successors. Once in-laws have been designated successors, resist the urge to meddle. They tend to work better with a "hands-off" mode. Be generally available, though, should they need advice. Balance, again, may be the key. In-laws are part of the family, yet in some sense, they are not. Treat them fairly as you would outside employees, and yet care for them as you would your own children.

The Entry of Professionals

The five companies have varying relationships with professionals. Generally, professionals can enter the business if they are trusted by the founder, and there are no eligible successors in the family. However, if family relationships and relationships with employees are not good, the company will not hire professionals.

Involving Professionals

Only two companies have professionals in management positions: Paeng Gapuz is the finance manager and Tito Gomez is the production manager of Snackfood Delights; three senior managers and all the branch managers of Gochiamco Groceries, Inc. are nonfamily members.

Only one family, however, is amenable to having senior managers on the board: Paeng and Tito are currently members of the board of Snackfood Delights. All the professionals are considered eligible successors by the founder and their eligibility virtually equal to that of the founder's own child.

The common thread in these two cases is the trust extended by the founder/owner to the nonfamily managers. Paeng and Tito have been with the snackfood company for more than 20 years, and have generally been given a free hand by Emilio in their own divisions.

This finding is compatible with Filipino norms of making outsiders "feel at home" in the business. Our vaunted hospitality is extended not only to kin, but also to colleagues and *kababayan* (townmate, fellow countryman). Unlike in Western conglomerates, where trust is not mentioned (only professionalism), many Asian companies rely on a more "human" code. Trust, though, has to be merited and one way of earning it is by staying long enough in the firm (as in the case of Paeng and Tito in Snackfood Delights). Contrast this with the skilled American professional managers who can be pirated on the basis of financial perks dangled in front of them.

These two situations also tie in with Davis's (1990) observation on the main reasons why professionals enter family firms: They get exposed to a wide range of decision-making situations; they acquire the power to get things done quickly; and they can interact with the owner himself.

Aside from enhancing the workforce and contributing to the growth of the firm, these professionals often act as trainors for the founder's children. Helen Chua trained (and is still training) with an outsider—a professional. This relieves the founder from charges of nepotism and allows his daughter to learn other strategies aside from his own. Recall that in-laws can be good trainors for the founder's offspring. If there are no capable in-laws, professionals can do just as good a job.

Although professionals and owners share effective working relations, they do not overstep and treat their bosses with familiarity—unless the latter wants it that way. Although hesitant at first, Paeng and Tito now go out to dinner with Emilio, who insists on it.

I find this surprising, as paradoxically, some management books (especially recent ones on "humanizing the workplace") encourage the founder to be "more friendly" with his employees to the extent of going out drinking or carousing with them. In fact, many American companies are trying now to emulate the Japanese practice of employees going out partying with the boss all night.

This does not seem to be the standard practice elsewhere in Asia, though. The only conclusion I can make here is that even if the relationship between founder and professional is excellent, it does not have to preclude respect and hierarchy. In the Asian context, status differential between leader and follower is an accepted order of nature. The business sphere is not an exception.

The relationship between professional managers and other employees depends on the period the managers were brought in. There was no problem with Snackfood Delights because Paeng and Tito entered the company at an early stage, and helped Emilio run it hence.

Professionals were brought in because the owner wanted to expand but found no suitable heir (the daughter was still in school). Even some of those working in businesses which are still wholly controlled by families feel this way, though they insist that professionals can only go up to a certain level. This is the case with Quality Shoes. Although the Perez couple mistrust outsiders, their sons are amenable to the idea of hiring professionals.

On the other hand, where relationships among family members and employees are not optimal, the entry of professionals may not be a desired option, as in the case of the Gotongs.

Companies which have hired or are thinking of hiring professionals have generally agreed to go public. Snackfood Delights is in the process of doing so. Most of them, however, have to ensure that the family retains a controlling interest as in the case of the Gochiamcos, the Perezes, and the Hernandezes.

The companies' varying relationships with professionals are summarized below.

Presence of professionals
- Paeng Gapuz and Tito Gomez/Snackfood Delights
- Three senior managers and all middle and junior managers/ Gochiamco Groceries, Inc.

No professionals at present, but family amenable to their entry
- Hernandez/Quality Shoes
- Perez/Excellence Printers

No professionals at present, and family not amenable to their entry
- Possibly Gotong/Garments House

Keeping and Maintaining Professionals

Continuity is often the litmus test of the succession in a family firm. Unless the family business is blessed with a number of capable heirs who work collaboratively, the presence of outsiders may be a requirement.

There are distinct advantages professionals bring into the firm. From the founder being almost always the sole power, decision-making becomes more shared. The founder usually operates by gut feel and intuition whereas professionals can bring in the element of planning. Product lines can diversify, uncertainty better dealt with, the process of change does not appear formidable at all. From a stance of "I know what to do," the company steadily grows into "Let's find out the answer" (Jaffe 1990).

To build and maintain a good professional-owner relationship, we offer some guidelines.

Treat outsiders with respect. It may be difficult for them to enter a firm wherein the employees normally side with the founder. Make responsibilities and boundary lines clear. Discuss with professionals what is expected of them, and once an agreement has been reached, stay clear. Give them time to accomplish their goals in their own way. Avoid playing one professional against another, as this may promote rivalry and absorb the professionals' energy as they try to please the founder rather than make the business work.

If family members have no violent objections, it may be a good idea to bring outsiders in before a crisis occurs. In this way, a more stable relationship can be formed and when a problem does arise, it can be attacked with less anxiety.

Mancuso and Shulman (1991) use the same reasoning to argue for the establishment of nonfamily feedback mechanisms:

> This idea is somewhat opposite to entrepreneurial logic. When things are apparently going smoothly, why change them? If it ain't broke, it don't need fixin'. But that's not true in family business. Like raising money for the business, the best time to raise capital is when you are not trapped in a lack-of-capital emergency. Although it sounds illogical at first, it is actually logical.

Treat professionals as "family" without compromising objectivity and other standards of fairness. The family business is not an impersonal concern—that is one of its strengths. Many management books have long advocated that business associates be treated "professionally," that is, impersonally. Yet, as we have seen, many successful businesses here do flourish because outsiders are treated as part of the family. This is certainly not easy. Silos (1991, 151) describes this dilemma:

> The family firm is extended to include all members of the organization as family. It is probably the most difficult part of the interphase between the family firm and family system. It means not only that the family must accept nonfamily members as family (to share in its privileges) but nonfamily members must accept the responsibility of being family (share in the responsibility of handling the business).

Yet, treating them as "family" does not mean completely eschewing respect for hierarchical lines. If cultural norms make such actions uncomfortable, tread the middle ground. Extend trust and care but not familiarity which may literally breed contempt later on.

There are no clear guidelines here, but I think a rule-of-thumb may suffice: Treat professionals not as acquaintances nor as blood relatives but as friends.

Successful Family Equals Successful Business

Finally, we summarize the functioning of the five families in both the personal and work areas in the table below.

Family/ Business	Family Functioning	Business Functioning
Chua/ Snackfood Delights	Low adequate (4)	Optimal (2)
Gochiamco/Gochiamco Groceries, Inc.	Optimal (2)	Optimal (2)
Gotong/ Garments House	Low borderline (8)	Midrange (5-6)
Hernandez/ Quality Shoes	High adequate (3)	Adequate (3-4)
Perez/ Excellence Printers	Low adequate (4)	Adequate (3-4)

What can we generally conclude? We can say that the health and competence ratings coincide with the family's level of individuation, use of power, nuclear alliances, and to some extent, extended relationships. The presence of professionals is often linked with company expansion.

Generally, if family health is optimal, so is business health. The Gochiamcos, the Hernandezes, the Perezes, even the Chuas are successful in both, albeit in varying degrees.

Most have individuated as much as the circumstances allow, with an egalitarian power structure, or if not, at least a clear one, with moderate dominance and relatively open communication lines and generally close and loving marital, parent-child, and sibling relationships. They usually welcome outsiders, be they in-laws or professionals.

(The Gochiamcos prefer to keep in-laws out of the business, but one is in the board and does fit in nicely. Professionals, however, are allowed to hold up to senior management positions only. The Hernandezes prefer not to have professionals in the business, but welcome capable in-laws.)

Although far from ideal, we can surmise from one of the cases studied here that it is still possible to have a successful company even if family relationships are fair at best. The Gotongs illustrate this. However, there's a caveat, as existing difficulties and unresolved problems in their family lives have spilled over into the business. The Gotongs, who are barely civil to each other, have magnified their childhood sibling rivalry with tragic results.

What can we generalize here? This finding emerges from all the five cases: Successful families lead to successful businesses, but not necessarily the other way around. In the long run, these businesses may encounter major problems brought on by familial ones.

We have come to realize that succession is a multifaceted issue linked to all the other factors. A good transition generally comes hand-in-hand with full individuation of parents and children, egalitarian decision-making by the family, cohesive and loving marital and sibling alliances, smooth relationships with in-laws, professionals, and other outsiders. The Gochiamcos are an excellent case study in this aspect.

SFI scores have generally coincided with observational ratings. This implies that even the most dysfunctional families are still realistic about their situation. This gives great hope for therapy.

Considering the responses to the interviews and the observation results, we can make one general observation: A healthy family is, more often than not, the secret of a successful business.

Can family and business be kept separate? The answer is no.

However conscious members are of never overlapping these two spheres, they inevitably do. The families studied show that patterns formed in the family environment while the children are growing up (however unconscious) usually have parallels in the business. An effective way to deal with this is to acknowledge that it is impossible to compartmentalize life and may not even be worth the effort.

Certainly, we are not implying that business should always be the topic over the dinner table or that bedroom quarrels be carried over to the boardroom. Nevertheless, dinner table topics can include positive aspects of the business which will expose the children early on and motivate them to join later. I also believe that if husband and wife kiss and make up in the bedroom, they will certainly carry on a more congenial relationship in the office the next day.

Filipino families are more closely knit than their Western counterparts. We may as well view this trait positively and put it to good use.

One aim, though implicit, of this study was to discover whether local families in business have to adopt Western approaches to succeed. Certainly, we have learned a lot from American and European methods, but do we have to adopt them at the cost of our own ways of doing things? Family businesses in the West have long been attacked as conservative, uninnovative, unprofessional, cradles of nepotism and despotism, and so forth.

Yet, we have seen that family businesses often glow in a positive light. Outgrowths of the vision of daring men or women, family businesses have struggled to survive, expand, persevere. In the process they have been handed over to the next generation as, perhaps, the most precious legacy many of them can ever have.

As the world grows more and more interdependent with trade barriers eroding, the call is for greater economic cooperation and internationalism. The Japanese are now powerhouses of their own, having imitated the efficiency of the Germans of an age past. The Americans seek to learn from the Japanese who, in turn, avow that they, too, have things to discover. Westernization in Asia may indeed only be on the surface, as Westwood (1992, 417) observes:

Although [Western] forces are clearly present in the [Asian] region, it is not certain to what extent they have significantly altered the approach to organization and management. It may be the case that on the surface there is widespread adoption of Western business and management practices, but that in the detail of their application and interpretation, they are made to fit with prevailing traditional system and cultural values.

Filipinos are a blend of East and West and, thus, possess an identity all their own. Their burgeoning family businesses have the best of both worlds to choose from in continuing to be the main engine of the country's economic growth.

Appendix 1

DEMOGRAPHIC QUESTIONNAIRE

This questionnaire is given to family members currently in the business and to nonfamily members in decision-making positions (at least at the managerial level). Note that #2 does not apply to nonfamily members.

Please state your

1. name
2. position in the family
3. title and position in the company
4. age
5. educational background
6. length of stay in the company
7. previous jobs (if any) in the company
8. shares (if any) in the company
9. reasons for joining the company
10. personal expectations/goals for the company

(In the case studies, names and other identifying factors have been altered.)

Appendix 2

INTERVIEW GUIDE QUESTIONS

[Family members involved in the company and nonfamily members in decision-making positions are interviewed in-depth. Actual interview questions may vary, of course, depending on the flow of the conversation but essentially the following are kept in mind as guides.]

1. Think about critical events which happened to your family within the last 10 years. What happened? How did you cope?

   Think about critical events which happened to your business within the last 10 years (or earlier). What happened? How did the company cope?

2. Who makes most of the decisions in the family? Is decision-making shared? How do you feel about this? (Think about decisions concerning marriage, moving house, etc.)

   How is decision-making done in the company? Is it shared? How do you feel about this? (Think about decisions concerning product development, expanding, succession, etc.)

3. Do in-laws have a say in decision-making in the company? How about outsiders (friends, business partners, etc.)? How do you feel about this?

4. Who are you closest to in the family? What accounts for this? What do you think are the benefits of such closeness? Any possible advantages?

   Who are you closest to in the company? What experiences have you shared? Any benefits [from] such closeness? Any possible disadvantages?

5. Are there any family members you do not feel close to? Why?

   Is there someone in the company you find difficult to work with? Why?

6. Who among the other family members do you see as close? What experiences do they share?

   Do you know of company members who work exceptionally well together? Cite instances.

7. Are there family members who do not get along very well? Why?

   Do you know of company members who do not get along? Cite instances.

8. How were the children raised in your family? Is creativity encouraged? How?

    How did you train your children to work for the business? Do you think it is a good idea for children to work in some other company before joining the business? How are they treated in the business?

9. Do you discuss business over the dinner table? During family outings? Do you discuss family matters in the office?

10. Name your personal goals. Are you on your way to achieving them? What do you want to do when you retire?

    Name some goals you have for your family. Are you on your way to achieving them?

    Name some goals you have for the business. Are you on your way to achieving them? Does the business have a succession plan? Why or why not? Explain.

11. Name a family you admire. Why do you admire them? Name a company you admire. Why do you admire [it]?

12. What is your personal philosophy? Describe. What is your company philosophy? Describe.

Appendix 3

SELF-REPORT FAMILY INVENTORY (SFI) VERSION II

For each question, mark the answer that best fits how you see your family now. If you feel that your answer is between two of the labeled numbers (the odd numbers), then choose the even number that is between them.

		Yes: Fits our family very well		Some: Fits our family		No: Does not fit our family
1.	Family members pay attention to each other's feelings.	1	2	3	4	5
2.	Our family would rather do things together than with other people.	1	2	3	4	5
3.	We all have a way in family plans.	1	2	3	4	5
4.	The grownups in this family understand and agree on family decisions.	1	2	3	4	5
5.	Grownups in the family compete and fight with each other.	1	2	3	4	5

		Yes: Fits our family very well	Some: Fits our family	No: Does not fit our family
6.	There is closeness in my family but each person is allowed to be special and different.	1 2	3	4 5
7.	We accept each other's friend.	1 2	3	4 5
8.	There is confusion in our family because there is no leader.	1 2	3	4 5
9.	Our family members touch and hug each other.	1 2	3	4 5
10.	Family members put each other down.	1 2	3	4 5
11.	We speak our minds, no matter what.	1 2	3	4 5
12.	In our home, we feel loved.	1 2	3	4 5
13.	Even when we feel close, our family is embarrassed to admit it.	1 2	3	4 5
14.	We argue a lot and never solve problems.	1 2	3	4 5
15.	Our happiest times are at home.	1 2	3	4 5

	Yes: Fits our family very well		Some: Fits our family		No: Does not fit our family
16. The grownups in this family are strong leaders.	1	2	3	4	5
17. The future looks good to our family.	1	2	3	4	5
18. We usually blame one person in our family if things aren't going right.	1	2	3	4	5
19. Family members go their own way most of the time.	1	2	3	4	5
20. Our family is proud of being close.	1	2	3	4	5
21. Our family is good at solving problems together.	1	2	3	4	5
22. Family members easily express warmth and caring toward each other.	1	2	3	4	5
23. It's okay to fight and yell in our family.	1	2	3	4	5
24. One of the adults in this family has a favorite child.	1	2	3	4	5
25. When things go wrong, we blame each other.	1	2	3	4	5
26. We say what we think and feel	1	2	3	4	5

	Yes: Fits our family very well		Some: Fits our family		No: Does not fit our family
26. We say what we think and feel.	1	2	3	4	5
27. Our family members would rather do things with other people than together.	1	2	3	4	5
28. Family members pay attention to each other and listen to what is said.	1	2	3	4	5
29. We are sorry about hurting each other's feelings.	1	2	3	4	5
30. The mood in my family is usually sad and blue.	1	2	3	4	5
31. We argue a lot.	1	2	3	4	5
32. One person controls and leads the family.	1	2	3	4	5
33. My family is happy most of the time.	1	2	3	4	5
34. Each person takes responsibility for his/her behavior.	1	2	3	4	5

35. On a scale of 1 to 5, I would
    rate my family as:

1	2	3	4	5

    My family functions well together.

    My family does not function well together at all. We really need help.

36. On a scale of 1 to 5, I would
    rate the independence in my
    family as:

1	2	3	4	5

    No one is independent. There are no open arguments. Family members rely on each other for satisfaction rather than on outsiders.

    Sometimes independent. There are some disagreements. Family members find satisfaction both within and outside of the family.

    Family members usually go their own way. Disagreements are open. Family members look outside of the family for satisfaction.

SOURCE: Beavers, W. R. and R. B. Hampson. 1990. *Successful families: Assessment and intervention*, 205-206. New York: W. W. Norton. Adapted by permission.

References Cited

Adler, A. 1928. Characteristics of the 1st, 2nd and 3rd child. *Children 3* (5): 14.

Adler, N. J. 1988. *International dimensions of organizational behavior.* Boston: Kent.

Alcorn, Pat B. 1982. *Success and survival in the family-owned business.* New York: McGraw Hill Book Co.

Alfonso, F. B. 1988. Managing family owned corporations: Mixing water and oil? *The Asian Manager* 1 (3): 4-8.

Andolfi, M. 1979. *Family therapy: An interactional approach.* New York: Plenum Press.

Bailey, D. and R. J. Simeonson. 1988. *Family assessment and early intervention.* New York: Merill.

Band, D. 1992. Corporate governance: Why agency theory is not enough? *European Management Journal* 10: 453-59.

Bank, S. and M. D. Kahn. 1975. Sisterhood-brotherhood is powerful: Sibling subsystems in family therapy. *Family Process* 14 (3): 311-37.

Baum, J. 1994. What nerve? *Far Eastern Economic Review* (November): 80-82.

Beavers, W. R. and R. B. Hampson. 1990. *Successful families: Assessment and intervention.* New York: W. W. Norton.

Beckhard, R. and W. G. Dyer. 1983. Managing continuity in the family-owned business. *Organizational dynamics* (n.p.).

Belleza, A. E. et al.1995. Philippines, Inc.: The next generation. Special report. *Businessworld* (April).

Blau, P. M. 1964. *Exchange and power in social life.* New York: Wiley.

Bloom, B. L. 1985. A factor analysis of self-report measures of family functioning. *Family Process* 24 (2): 225-39.

Boissenvain, J. 1974. *Friends of friends: Networks, manipulators, and coalitions.* New York: St. Martin's Press.

Bossard, J. H. S. and E. S. Boll. 1960. *The sociology of child development.* New York: Harper.

Bowen, M. 1972. Toward the differentiation of a self in one's own family. In *Family Interaction*, ed. J. Framo. New York: Harper.

_____. Theory in the practice of psychotherapy. In *Family therapy*, ed. P. Guerin. New York: Gardner.

_____. 1978. *Family therapy in clinical practice.* New York: Aronson.

Caplow, T. 1968. *The sociology of work.* Minneapolis: Minneapolis University Press.

Carandang, M. L. A. 1987. *Filipino children under stress: Family dynamics and therapy.* Quezon City: Ateneo de Manila University Press.

Caruncho, E. R. III. 1976. "A corporate strategy for a family owned construction corporation." Master's thesis, Asian Institute of Management.

Castro, M. C. 1992. "Families with terminally ill children: An exploratory study of family dynamics." Master's thesis, Ateneo de Manila University.

Clifford, M. 1994. Heir force. *Far Eastern Economic Review* (November): 78-79.

Cohen, A. R. 1974. *Tradition, change and conflict in Indian family business.* Netherlands: Institute of Social Studies.

247

Covey, S. R. 1989. *The seven habits of highly effective people.* New York: Simon and Schuster.

Danco, K. 1981. *From the other side of the bed: A woman looks at life in the family business.* Ohio: The University Press.

Davis, J., M. Gallo, and P. Leach. 1990. Nonfamily managers. Paper read in "Leading the family business." Seminar conducted by the Owner Managed Business Institute.

Donnelly, R. G. 1964. The family business. *Harvard Business Review* 42 (4): 93-105.

Dyer, W. G. 1986. *Cultural change in family firms: Anticipating and managing business and family transitions.* San Francisco: Jossey-Bass.

Ehrenfeld, T. 1995. The new and improved American small business. *Incorporated* 17 (January): 34-45.

Estess, P. S. 1994. Out of order. *Entrepreneur* 22 (6): 68-71.

Fenn, D. 1994. Are your kids good enough to run the business? *Incorporated* (August): 36-48.

Fritz, R. 1992. *The entrepreneurial family: How to sustain the vision and value in your family business.* New York: McGraw-Hill.

Garcia, R. V. 1973. "Corporate strategy for a Filipino family corporation." Master's thesis, Asian Institute of Management.

Green, R. G., M. S. Kolevzon, and N. R. Vosler. 1985. The Beavers-Timberlawn model of family competence and the circumplex model of family adaptability and cohesion: Separate but equal. *Family Process* 24 (3): 385-98.

Gurman, A. S. and D. P. Knishkern, 1980. *Handbook of family therapy.* New York: Brunner/Mazel.

Haley, J. 1962. Family experiments: A new type of experimentation. *Family Process* 1: 265-93.

Haley, J. 1976. *Problem-solving therapy.* San Francisco: Jossey-Bass.

Hansen, J. C. and L. L'Abate. 1982. *Approaches to family therapy.* New York: MacMillan.

Henson, J. 1975. "Enterprise strategies for a Filipino family with business interests in the transportation industry." Master's thesis, Asian Institute of Management.

Herbert, M. 1988. *Working with children and their families.* London: Routledge Limited.

Holloman, C. R. 1986. Headship vs. leadership. *Business and Economic Review*, 32 (2): 35-37.

Ihinger, M. 1975. The referee role and norms of equity: A contribution toward a theory of sibling conflict. *Journal of Marriage and the Family* 37 (3): 515-24.

Jaffe, D. T. 1990. *Working with the ones you love: Conflict resolution and problem-solving strategies for a successful family business.* California: Conari Press.

Jung, M. 1984. Structural family therapy: Its application to Chinese families. *Family Process* 23: 365-74.

Kazdin, A. E. 1992. *Research design in clinical psychology,* 2d ed. New York: MacMillan.

Kerr, M. E. 1981. Family systems theory and therapy. In *Handbook of family therapy,* eds. A. Gurman and D. P. Kniskern. New York: Brunner/Mazel.

Lank, A. G. 1992. Cultures in families and family companies. Paper read in "Leading the family business." Seminar conducted by the International Institute for Management Development.

Lansberg, I. S. 1983. Managing human resources in family firms: The problem of institutional overlap. *Organizational Dynamics* (Summer): 39-46.

Latts, S. M. 1966. The four-fold, equi-sexed, intact family: Its organization and interactional patterns. Doctoral dissertation, University of Minnesota.

Levinson, H. 1971. Conflicts that plague family businesses. *Harvard Business Review* 49 (2): 90-98.

Lee, C. 1988. Theories of family adaptability: Toward a synthesis of Olson's circumsplexa and the Beavers systems models. *Family Process* 27: 73-96.

Leibenstein, H. 1987. *Inside the firm: The inefficiencies of hierarchy*. Massachusetts: Harvard University Press.

Limlingan, V. S. 1986. *The overseas Chinese in ASEAN: Business strategies and management practices*. Pasig: Vita Development Corporation.

Liwag, E. C. D. 1987. *Families of autistic children: An exploratory study of their stress and coping experiences*. Master's thesis, Ateneo de Manila Graduate School of Business.

Malone, S. C. and P. V. Jenster, 1991. The problem of the plateaued owner-manager. Paper read in "Leading the family business." Seminar conducted by the International Institute for Management Development.

Mancuso, J. R. and N. Shulman. 1991. *Running a family business*. New York: Prentice-Hall.

MacCandless, B. R. 1969. Childhood socialization. In *Handbook of socialization theory and research*, ed. D. A. Goslin. Chicago: Rand McNally.

Menchik, P. L. 1980. Primogeniture, equal sharing, and the U. S. distribution of wealth. *Quarterly Journal of Economics* 94: 299-316.

Minuchin, S. 1987. *Families and family therapy*. Massachusetts: Harvard University Press.

Miranda, B. T. G. 1991. *The Filipino family*. Quezon City: University of the Philippines Press.

Negandhi, A. R. 1973. *Management and economic development: The case of Taiwan*. The Hague: Martinus Nijhoff.

Nisperos, M. K. G. 1994. The world of the scavenger child: A phenomenological and in-depth clinical study of some scavenger children on Smokey Mountain. Master's thesis, Ateneo de Manila University.

Olson, D. H., D. H. Sprenkle, and C. S. Russell. 1979. Circumplex model of marital family types and clinical applications. *Family Process* 18 (1): 3-28.

Olson, D. H. and R. E. Cromwell. *Power in families*. New York: Wiley.

Papero, D. V. 1983. Family systems theory and therapy. In *Handbook of family and marital therapy*, ed. B. Woman and G. Stricker. New York: Plenum Press.

Quintos, M. V. 1992. Case studies on family corporation. Master's thesis, Ateneo de Manila Graduate School of Business.

Raven, B. H., R. Centers, and A. Rodrigues. 1975. The bases of conjugal power. In *Power in families*, ed. R. E. Cromwell and D. H. Olson. New York: Wiley.

Redding, S. G. 1990. *The spirit of Chinese capitalism*. New York: Walter de Gruyter.

Robinson, R. D. 1964. *International business policy*. New York: Holt, Rinehart, and Winston.

Rosenblatt, P. C. et al. 1985. *The family in business*. San Francisco: Jossey-Bass.

Rueveni, U. 1979. *Networking families in crisis*. New York: Human Sciences Press.

Schvaneveldt, J. D. and M. Ihinger. 1979. Sibling relationships in the family. In *Contemporary theories about the family: Research-based theories* 1, eds. W. R. Buss et al. New York: Free Press.

Silos, L. R. (n.d.). The business firm: The bureaucracy and the clan. Discussion paper no. 93-20. Germany: Zentrum fur Europaische.

_____. 1991. Oikos: *The two faces of organization*. Manila: Asian Institute of Management.

Silverman, G. 1994. Almost family. *Far Eastern Economic Review* (November): 85-86.

Sonnenfeld, J. 1988. *The hero's farewell*. Oxford: University Press.

Speck, R. and C. Attneave. 1973. *Family Networks*. New York: Vintage Books.

Speer, D. 1970. Family systems: Morphostasis and morphogenesis or "Is homeostasis enough?" *Family Proceedings* 9: 259-78.

Stierlin, H. 1974. *Separating parents and adolescents*. New York: Quadrangle.

Tiglao, R. 1994. Not strictly flamenco. *Far Eastern Economic Review* (November): 82-84.

Toman, W. 1961. *Family constellation: Its effects on personality and social behavior*. New York: Springer.

Tu, I. C. 1991. Family enterprises in Taiwan. In *Business networks and economic development in East and Southeast Asia*, ed. G. Hamilton. Centre of Asian Studies, University of Hong Kong.

Tuason, M. T. G. 1992. Five urban poor families with alcoholic fathers: A clinically-descriptive and exploratory study. Master's thesis, Ateneo de Manila University.

Vancil, R. F. 1987. Passing the baton: *Managing the process of CEO succession*. Boston: Harvard Business School.

Ward, J. L. (n. d.). Developing strategy in the family business. Paper read in "Leading the family business." Seminar conducted by the International Institute for Management Development.

Westwood, R. T., ed. 1992. *Organizational behavior: Southeast Asian perspective*. Hong Kong: Longman.

Williams, L. E. 1952. Chinese entrepreneurs in Indonesia. *Explorations in entrepreneurial history* 5 (1): 34-60.

Wynne, L. C. 1958. Pseudo mutuality in the family relation of schizophrenics. *Psychiatry* 21:205-22.

Yoo, S. and S. M. Lee. 1987. Management style and practice of Korean chaebols. *California Management Review* 29 (4): 95-110.

Zuk, G. 1972. *Family therapy: A triadic-based approach*. New York: Behavioral Publications.

Index